8.95

D1190464

NEW PERSPECTIVES IN SOCIOLOGY

Edited by John Wakeford

This series provides an opportunity for young sociologists to present original material and also to summarise and review critically certain key themes and controversies in their subject. All the authors are experts in their own field and each monograph not only provides in an accessible form stimulating ideas for the specialist but also represents in itself a significant personal contribution to the discipline.

Students of sociology will find the series invaluable. For non-specialists the monographs provide a clear and authoritative insight into the concerns and perspectives of the modern sociologist.

The Sociology
of the Professions

PHILIP ELLIOTT

HERDER AND HERDER

1972

HERDER AND HERDER NEW YORK
232 Madison Avenue, New York 10016

Library of Congress Catalog Card Number: 75-188934

© Philip Elliott 1972

Printed in Great Britain

For my mother

Contents

Preface

It is now nearly forty years since Carr-Saunders and Wilson completed their comprehensive work on the British professions. This book is not intended to replicate their empirical survey but to provide a sociological survey of recent writing and research on professions and professionalism. The aim is to review the main issues which have exercised sociologists, to contrast the various perspectives and approaches used and to point the way towards further development in the field.

It does not seem too much of an exaggeration to say that increasing interest in the sociology of the professions has been accompanied by a growing sterility in the subject. This has been partly due to a preoccupation with the form of professional phenomena and partly due to the way in which the field has been dominated by small-scale empirical studies and *a priori* statements about the structure and function of professions. The energy which has gone into the empirical work could well be channelled, as in some cases it already has, towards more interesting and significant questions about the organisation of professions and the behaviour of professionals. These in turn would have wider implications for assessing the place of professions in society and professionalism in the social culture. The gradual routinisation of the sociology of the professions has meant that these wider horizons have largely slipped from view.

Initially my interest in this subject was awakened during the time I spent at the Department of Sociology and Social Anthropology in the University of Manchester. I am particularly indebted to David Morgan, who supervised my work there, and to Professor Peter Worsley, Colin Lacey and Bryan Roberts. I am also grateful to my colleagues at the Centre for Mass Communication Research for help and collaboration in various studies which while only tangentially related to the subject of this book have played a large part in crystallising my ideas on the subject. I am indebted to John Wakeford for continual encouragement and for commenting helpfully on an earlier draft. I am also grateful to the secretarial staff at the Centre for patiently typing successive versions of the manuscript.

PHILIP ELLIOTT

Leicester, 1971

1 Introduction

It is one of the clichés of history that the middle classes are always rising. The expansion of professional occupations within the middle class has given a new form to this perpetual historical motion. The growth in the number of professionals and in the number of occupations claiming professional status is one of a number of current processes of social change which have been examined by sociologists. Among these processes professionalisation has received relatively little attention. It would be unreasonable to expect a literature on the sociology of the professions as large as that on urban or industrial sociology. Most people live in cities and work in industry. Nearly a tenth of the employed population of Great Britain and a rather larger proportion of the employed population in the United States of America are members of what the respective census authorities loosely define as professional occupations.[1] The rapid increase in the number of people in such occupations is one indication of the importance of the process of professionalisation. A more important reason is that this process is closely linked with various other aspects of social change. The study of professions and professionalism provides a focal point which can show the interconnections between a number of apparently different developments.

One aim of this book is to show how sociological interest in professions and professionals can take us beyond a study of particular occupations into a more general analysis of change in the social structure. To achieve this a crucial distinction must be drawn between professional occupations in pre-industrial and post-industrial society.[2] Although in both cases professions were occupations of the middle or upper class, the change in the nature of professionalism was paralleled by a change in the nature of the class system. The point is taken up in greater detail in Chapter 2. Alongside the development of an industrial economy there also emerged a more rigorous and extensive occupational system. This system was supported by the growth of technical knowledge, the

expansion of education and changes in the function of the education system. The relationship between these changes and the
recruitment, selection and training of professionals is taken up
below in Chapter 3.

At various points the process of professionalisation coincides
with the process of bureaucratisation identified by Weber.[3] This
overlap is most obvious in the increase in specialised functionaries
within complex organisations. Within industry the growth of professional occupations can be seen as one aspect of the separation
of ownership and control.[4] These remarks beg the question of
whether professionalism is possible outside the individual practice
situation of the traditional professions. Chapter 4 returns to this
question in a general analysis of professional practice and organisation in different types of work situation. Occupational specialisation and technical change have also affected the structure of
knowledge in society. The distribution of knowledge is, itself, liable
to become a specialised function. Segmentalised development of
knowledge poses particular problems for its control and use, problems to which we shall return in the final chapter of this book. The
argument here is not that professionalism is a prime cause of any
of these developments, but that it is involved in all of them.

This sketch of a place for the sociology of the professions within
a general examination of changes in the social structure assumes
that it is possible to agree on a definition of the subject-matter; to
agree on what is a profession. Some have argued that profession
cannot be considered a useful category in sociology, because it
lacks a distinct referent.[5]

This very imprecision has at least one beneficial consequence.
Professional and non-professional occupations share many common characteristics. It is difficult to point to a sharp dividing line
between the two. Because of this the study of professions and
professionals can throw light on a number of issues in the sociology
of work and occupations.[6] It is a second aim of this book to elucidate some of these issues; to show, for example, what an analysis
of professions and professionals can tell us about the relationship
between work and other areas of social life. To achieve this second
aim it will be necessary to complement the structural analysis of
social change with an examination of the place of work in the life
of the individual.

The name 'profession' is widely and imprecisely applied to a

2

variety of occupations. The adjective 'professional' is even more overworked, extending, for example, to cover the opposite of amateur and the opposite of a botched job, two concepts which need not be synonymous. One of the tasks of the sociologist is to develop concepts and categories which will assist an explanation of the organisation of society and the behaviour of people within it. One source of such categories are the classifications already in use in everyday life, but the task of classification cannot end there. Indeed, starting from that point may lead to an endless process of verbal juggling to make the category, and the phenomenon, fit for both scientific and everyday purposes.

Cogan, in his second attempt to reach a definition of a profession,[7] pointed out that the differences between the definitions of other authors were largely to be explained by the different purposes which they had had in putting forward their definitions. He distinguished three types of definition : persuasive definitions, designed to argue the case for a particular occupation; operational definitions, used to facilitate decisions about the organisations and practice of an occupation; and logistic definitions, which were descriptive attempts to draw verbal boundaries round historical material and customary usage. Historical material and customary usage have proved difficult to restrict within the confines of such verbal boundaries.

Faced with this problem, some sociologists have concluded that profession is a term of little scientific value. Everett Hughes, for example, discussing the work of Real Estate Agents, concluded that his initial question – 'Are they professional?' – had only served to distract him.[8] He suggests that profession is a symbolic label for a desired status. In consequence he should have asked another question, namely, 'When do people begin to apply this label to themselves?' Elsewhere, Hughes has included professions as a distinct category in two occupation typologies based on different personality characteristics and different types of work relationship.[9] Habenstein, however, has advanced a similar argument to abandon the concept of profession as no more than a status claim.[10] Habenstein likens it to a number of other concepts, for example, 'crime', 'family' and 'urban', which have also given rise to similar problems of 'terminological clarification'. It would be more difficult to obtain ready agreement to discard the other concepts on this list.

Habenstein's list does not include 'class', but it very well might. The comparison with the concept of class shows, not only that the same concept can be analysed as a symbol at the same time as it is used as an analytic device,[11] but also that analytic concepts in social research rarely have distinct and unambiguous referents. This does not invalidate a concept any more than the fact that all trees differ from each other invalidates the use of the general term 'tree'.

Problems of definition in social research can often be seen as a version of the old philosophical problem of universals. They are based on much the same question, namely, what empirical reality do general terms describe? One familiar resolution of this problem was put forward by Plato. The quest for a watertight definition of a profession seems to be based on the same premises as Plato's solution to the philosophical problem. It is a quest for an empirical ideal which can only exist in a Platonic heaven. Whatever characteristics are chosen for the definition, any candidate for membership of the category can only fill the bill more or less, never completely. But this does not make the concept useless, providing it will mark out phenomena which share typical relationships with the rest of their environment, and which typically organise their own activities in the same way.

These two properties seem to be the key requirements of an ideal type of profession and professional. Weber used the ideal type method to draw attention to a key feature of social relationships and then to follow through the consequences which it had for other aspects of social organisation.

> In all cases, rational or unrational, sociological analysis abstracts from reality and, at the same time, helps us to understand it, in that it shows with what degree of approximation a concrete historical phenomenon can be subsumed under one or more of these concepts . . . it is probably seldom if ever that a real phenomenon can be found which corresponds exactly to one of these ideally constructed pure types.[12]

The ideal type method allows us to identify a social phenomenon, and to examine the part it plays within the general social structure, instead of simply isolating it for individual inspection. The third aim of this book is to contribute to such an ideal type

4

of professional behaviour and organisation and to outline its place within social structure and process.

It remains to explain why, in the case of the professions, so much energy has been expended in the argument over definitions. Many other common terms have been readily accepted without elaborate re-examination, but work on the sociology of the professions, in general or on particular professional occupations, seems inevitably to start with a definitional debate. Millerson has tabulated twenty-one definitions taken from some of the most celebrated works, showing that most are based on a few overlapping characteristics.[13] The recent report of the Monopolies Commission provides another addendum to this list.[14] Although the Commission argued that a definition was impractical and unnecessary it set out a list of necessary characteristics. The list covers familiar ground – a specialised skill and service, an intellectual and practical training, a high degree of professional autonomy and responsibility, a fiduciary relationship with the client, a sense of collective responsibility for the profession as a whole, an embargo on some methods of attracting business and an occupational organisation testing competence, regulating standards and maintaining discipline. Hickson and Thomas have recently gone to the trouble of developing a professionalisation scale based on a similar list of characteristics.[15] This scale applied to the British 'qualifying associations' at least had the advantage of face validity – the medical and legal corporations, the architects and civil engineers all scored highly.

One reason why the problem of definition looms so large is implicit in the previous discussion. The title 'profession' is a claim to social standing and recognition. Another reason, pointed out by Millerson, is the assumption that professionalism is a static phenomenon rather than a dynamic process. This dynamic process operates at three different levels, the level of general social change, the level of occupational organisation and the level of the individual life-cycle. This book will cover all three levels of analysis, discussing professionalisation as part of general social change, the way different occupations aspire to and achieve professional status and the way in which individuals become practising members of particular professions.

A third reason for the preoccupation with the problem of definition is that much of the central work on professions in society has been done within the tradition of British empiricism. The work of Carr-Saunders and Wilson provides a foundation stone for this approach to the subject.[16] They, themselves, eschewed the task of definition but they devoted a section of their study to a general review of the common features of different professional occupations. First, each of these occupations had been individually analysed in detail. Much of the interest in this type of approach is in the different histories of various occupations. The different features of various occupations became a subject of historical if not sociological interest, but at the same time they became a matter of definitional dispute.

Among sociological theories structural functionalism has been particularly important in attempting to give the professions a distinct role within the social structure. Emile Durkheim, attempting to cope with one of the major questions of sociology and social philosophy, how is order maintained within the social structure, suggested that the division of labour in society was itself functional for the maintenance of social cohesion.[17] He contrasted the mechanistic solidarity of pre-industrial communities in which the social institutions and the economic conditions together ensured that society was maintained through the similarity of life available to the people, with the scope for individualism and difference which had developed with industrial change and the division of labour. Division of labour had replaced a social order based on 'resemblances' and the all-pervasive enforcement of the 'collective type', with another form of social solidarity, the organic, based on the interdependence of different functions.

It is possible to dispute the detail of Durkheim's historical account of social change, but nevertheless his analysis raises important questions about the maintenance of society in spite of the divisions between specialised functions. Although Durkheim argued that organic solidarity was the normal consequence of the division of labour, he also recognised that abnormal forms might develop which would turn the division of labour into a divisive rather than a cohesive force. One of these in particular, the anomic form of the division of labour, he saw as a real threat to the social structure of his time.

The anomic form of the division of labour is a state of social conflict in which stability is maintained only by the interplay of power and interest groups within society. According to Durkheim,

6

it results from the separation of the different parts of the social structure. The interdependent parts lose contact with each other and it was that contact which had provided the basis for the normal form of organic solidarity. He saw the crises of the trade cycle as a product of this state of anomie. Manufacturers, for example, had no contact with their market so they were unable to recognise and predict the demand for which they were producing. The anomic form of the division of labour thus replaced a social equilibrium based on a moral order with an uneasy truce based on the balance between separate centres of power.

Durkheim added a new preface to the second edition of 'The Division of Labour in Society', entitled 'Some Notes on Occupational Groups'. In it he proposed his solution to this problem of anomie. Although this solution is not limited to an account of the role of professional occupational groups, Durkheim's argument is of particular interest for our purposes, both because it influenced the development of the structural functional approach to the study of professions, and because it posed clearly some of the important questions about occupational organisation and the links between specialised and separated occupational groups.

For Durkheim, the family seems to have been the paradigmatic social institution in which both organic solidarity and the division of labour were to be found. His hope was that the occupational group would develop a form like the family, but on a larger scale. It was to occupy a mid-point, between the State and the family, in the social structure. He suggests two parallels for this form of organisation, the medieval guilds and the Roman *Collegia*. In his account of both these historical forms he is at pains to stress their communal, corporate functions. According to Durkheim, while the family was the basic communal unit in the agricultural economy, the *collegia* or the guilds took over many of its functions in the craft economy.

He goes on to argue that the development of the industrial economy has converted economic activity from a minor and despised part of social life to the predominant activity. It is in business activity and the economic philosophy of *laissez-faire* that the problem of anomie can be seen most clearly. Some form of occupational organisation is, therefore, particularly necessary in business to provide a code of moral practice in

7

place of unrestrained economic interest. The form of organisation which Durkheim actually had in mind was not trade unions of workmen alone, but occupational corporations embracing both employers and employees, in much the same way as the medieval guilds included master craftsmen, journeymen and apprentices.

But Durkheim's prescription for the ills he identified is perhaps the least important part of his thesis. Although workers and employers may occasionally be united by common interests in their dealings with a third party such as the State, corporations of the sort which Durkheim suggested seem unlikely to develop because of the much more pervasive differences of interest within industry, even given the separation of ownership and control. The doctrines of guild socialism, which acquired a following in England after the First World War, bear some resemblance to Durkheim's, with the proviso that the guild socialists saw organisations of workers taking over the roles of employers and managers. It is particularly interesting that one ostensible reason for the rejection of guild socialism within the British Labour Party was the development of professionalism looked at from a different point of view. In discussing which method of nationalisation the Labour Party should adopt, a memorandum to the 1933 Party Conference declared that in industry 'the day-to-day administration is quickly becoming a profession, and the persons undertaking this work will have to be trained business administrators'.[18] Another and perhaps more significant argument against workers' control was the need for trade unions to retain their autonomy within industry if they were to represent their members effectively.

Guild socialism was just one of the models of society erected by theorists at the beginning of the twentieth century to counteract the dominance which business and capitalism seemed about to achieve within the social structure. Rothblatt has argued that the idea of professionalism was itself another such theory.[19] In his study of nineteenth-century Cambridge, Rothblatt shows how the idea of professionalism was advanced by the teachers of that university as a response to changes in the social structure which threatened the position of the university, and to changes in their own occupation and career patterns. The details of Rothblatt's study are more relevant to a later chapter, but his general argu-

8

ment has obvious application to Durkheim's thesis which we have just reviewed.

Durkheim thought that occupational corporations would create a moral and communal order to counter the anomie of industrial society. Others saw in profesionalism, and the ideal of altruistic service, a method of achieving similar ends. Carr-Saunders and Wilson, for example, argued that professional associations were stabilising elements within society. They looked to the growth of these associations to provide individuals with a sense of power and purpose, such as had not been achieved simply by giving them the right to vote.[20]

Particular stress in the inter-war period was laid on the contrast between business and the professions. This was a contrast between economic self-interest and altruistic service for limited rewards, between the profit motive and professional ethics.[21] As a contrast it seems to have been particularly relevant to the economic problems of the depression. At that time it was hard to show that the economy was naturally arranged to ensure that business served the community. Moreover, professional occupations had their own authoritative methods for achieving professional goals. It was obvious that something was wrong with business, but much less obvious what could be done about it, on its own terms. Both Carr-Saunders and Wilson and R. H. Tawney[22] thought that the increase in the number of salaried managers performing specialised functions was a sign of professionalism intruding into business itself. In common with others, they welcomed this development, though Tawney went further than most in spelling out his hopes for a professional reorganisation of the structure of capitalism.

But the emphasis on altruistic service and the contrast with business did not endure as the key characteristic attributed to professionalism. In 1939, Talcot Parsons published an influential paper suggesting that the similarities between professions and business were more important than their differences.[23] This was in spite of the fact that two years before Parsons had argued that professional and commercial attitudes were opposed and that '. . . encouragement of the professions is one of the most effective ways of promoting disinterestedness in contemporary society . . .'.[24] Parsons' new argument was that in terms of the pattern variables which he was developing for the analysis of social roles, business

9

and the professions shared the same characteristics. Both were rational, functionally specific and universalistic. Moreover, in both cases individuals pursued 'success', that is they played social roles according to the rules laid down within the social structure. Parsons accepted that there were important differences in the organisation of the two groups, but not in their motivation. Both altruism and acquisitiveness were false motivational assumptions when action took place within institutionally defined patterns of social roles.[25]

A new contrast appeared in the literature to replace that between business and the professions. This was between the free or 'liberal' tradition of the old professions and salaried professional employment by the State or large organisations. It seems hardly coincidental that this shift of emphasis coincided with the rise to prominence of Nazi Germany and Stalinist Russia followed by the solution of some of the major problems of capitalism first through war, and then through the managed economy.[26] The aspiring professional has not been the only one to use the term 'profession' with an ideological or symbolic connotation.

From Durkheim's general analysis of the function of occupational groups within society, structural-functional analysis has moved to a particular concern with professional occupations. Various reasons have been suggested for treating the professions as a special form of occupational organisation. Various particular social functions have been attributed to the professions. This type of functional analysis shares a problem with the descriptive approach discussed above. It is as hard to specify universally applicable functions as it is to detail the characteristics making up a universally valid definition. Following chapters will take up some of the variations within and between occupations commonly called professions.

For the present, the concern is with professionalism at the level of the social structure. Professionalism is one method through which the knowledge available to society is developed and used in the performance of specialised tasks. A number of arguments have been advanced to try to differentiate further some forms of knowledge and tasks as peculiarly professional. For example, Parsons[27] has suggested that professions have taken over tasks which were previously performed within the family. These tasks typically involve the management of social conflict, providing

10

the idea of social conflict is treated broadly enough to cover such cases as illness. This claim can be made to fit the traditional professions where the professional is approached by clients to resolve their problems. It has less obvious relevance to the growth of specialised scientific and technical groups whose functions were never performed within the family. However, in all cases of specialisation there is the problem of integrating the specialty with others in the performance of necessary tasks. The professional case is particularly interesting because of the tension between the ends and means developed within the professional specialty and the ends and means of other groups and institutions within society.

The separate identity of the professional group has been important in developing two themes of research in the sociology of the professions. One of these has started from the original insights of such authors as Sorokin and Whitehead[28] and investigated the way in which the thought and practice of various professional groups is related to their knowledge, skill and work situations.[29] But this study of professional ideologies is relatively undeveloped compared with the study of professions as separate social groups, in Goode's phrase 'as communities within a community'.[30]

The idea of professions as relatively separate groups within society is part of the more general structural functional approach to the study of professions.[31] The professional group controls a body of expert knowledge which is applied to specialised tasks. This poses special problems of social control. Such problems can be seen in the relationship between the professional and the unskilled client or, more generally, in the tension between values developed within the profession and the values of the wider society. Social control in the professional group takes two forms. The professional institutions oversee all the functions of the profession. They lay down standards controlling entry to the group. Through the training necessary to achieve these qualifications, and through associations with professional peers, the individual acquires the norms and values of the group. Through these, mechanisms of social control become internalised. Such internalisation is peculiarly necessary because of the opportunities which exist for exploitation in professional practice and because of the loose control which can be exercised by institutions, especially in individual practice situations.

11

This theory, which we shall have occasion to elaborate in the course of this book, has been particularly influential in suggesting research problems. One area of interest has been the study of various types of professional education to see when and how the norms and values of the occupational group are acquired. Studies have been made of the way in which individuals are recruited, selected and socialised into professional roles. Another subject of study has been the organisation of professional practice itself and the study of the professions as a separate group united in the performance of a common role. In this, case studies have concentrated on the process of professionalisation at the middle level, as a process of change in the institutions and organisation of particular occupational groups.

In the chapters which follow, studies based on the structural functional approach will be compared with studies using different perspectives. One aim of these comparisons will be to show that the structural functional theory is itself inadequate. The main point of criticism is that by concentrating on the supposed needs of the social system the theory, in many cases, has encouraged the acceptance of professional ideology at its face value. In reality the supposed needs may not be met, may be met by quite different mechanisms or may not be needs at all, in the sense that they do not impinge upon the social situation.

Nevertheless, the structural functional approach has drawn attention to problems of professionalisation at all three of the levels outlined earlier in this chapter. It raises questions about the nature of the professional group, the way the individual acquires membership of it, and about the integration and control of specialised functions within the social system. While we shall have occasion in the present study to take issue with many of the analyses offered at the first two levels, we shall also take as our point of departure professionalism as a method of managing specialisation within society. This is not to say it is the only method, or a method which manages completely to resolve conflict and ensure equilibrium. On the contrary, the more professions achieve the status of a community within a community, the more they are likely to have a divisive as well as a cohesive influence. By adopting this perspective, we shall be enabled to link the process of professionalisation more closely to some of the other areas of social change mentioned at the beginning of this chapter. We must now turn to a more detailed examination of the historical development and contemporary situation of the professions and professionalism.

2 The Development of the Professions in Britain

An Historical Perspective

Modern professionalism is a composite phenomenon, the product of a variety of different historical developments. In the course of this book an ideal type of professionalism will be developed to give the subject conceptual unity, but first an historical perspective is necessary to understand the way such an ideal type emerged and the form which it takes in different societies. Such a perspective is particularly necessary in Britain, to distinguish British professions from their American counterparts and to examine the way in which changes in professions and professionalism were interrelated with other processes of social change. The United States is a country with a small past and a large present. Much of the work on the contemporary situation in the sociology of the professions, discussed in later chapters, has been carried out there. But the course of social change which lies behind the present situation is more easily traced in the longer time-scale available in Britain.

Professional occupations in pre-industrial and post-industrial Britain differ sharply in their characteristics. Yet many of the features of the latter can be shown to have derived from earlier forms of occupational organisation, exemplified by the former. Such derivations are based on two main processes of change – the decline of status professionalism in which professions were relatively unimportant in the organisation of work or community services but occupied a niche high in the system of social stratification, and conversely the rise of occupational professionalism, based on specialisation of knowledge and task. The first of these processes directs attention to the place which professions occupy relative to other class and status groups in society. The second focuses on the part which professionalism plays in managing the division of labour and specialisation of knowledge. In Britain the develop-

14

ment of the second type of profession coincided with such other major processes of social change as industrial development and urban growth during the nineteenth century.

Both these processes of change in the professions were dependent on these more fundamental changes in the basic social and economic structure. The development of industrial technology and the market economy reversed the relationship between occupation and social status. In pre-industrial society those with highest status did not engage in work or have an occupation at all in the modern sense of a 'specific activity with a market value which an individual continually pursues for the purpose of obtaining a steady flow of income . . .'.[1]

Social position was based on traditional or political title, backed by inherited wealth, usually held in the form of land and property. The pre-industrial professions handled areas of life involving potential social problems and conflicts but their specific contributions to the economy and the social system were marginal. In many cases their specialised expertise was negligible or unrelated to the problems with which the profession professed to deal. Professionals were an appendage to the high-status groups in society at that time.

In modern society occupation itself has acquired a new significance as the key indicator of general social position. Few people have the means to live without working and there seems to be some compulsion even on those who can to take up some type of occupation. The activities of the Queen and the Royal Family, for example, are popularly evaluated in terms of the job they have to do. Many studies of the status system of industrial societies have concentrated on measuring the relative prestige of different occupations.[2] Occupation is commonly used as an indicator of status and, perhaps with less theoretical justification, as an indicator of class membership, in all sorts of sociological studies. It has acquired this significance as a social category because of the development of labour power as an important commodity in the exchange economy. Different types of occupation represent different forms of labour power.

This basic change in the place of occupations within the social structure has had an important impact on the professions and has made professionalism a central feature of modern social organisation. To a large extent the professions were unaffected by the initial process of industrial reorganisation. Technical change and economic rationalisation have only slowly been applied to personal services and professional tasks. Change in the professions developed independently through changes in the structure of knowledge and in the organisation of other social institutions with which the professions were associated. The Industrial Revolution did have an indirect impact on the market for professional services. In time the new middle class, drawing on new sources of industrial wealth, exercised powerful pressure on the educational and occupational systems for change to accommodate their needs. The growing importance of occupation as marketable labour power was reflected in the professions by a tendency towards specialisation of expertise and task.

This chapter will illustrate the way in which this general process of change influenced the professions and trace the development of modern professionalism, as a mixture of status professionalism and occupational specialisation. First, we shall show how the professions emerged as separate occupational groups and trace the relationships between the pre-industrial professions and the social élite of the time. The systems of recruitment and education which were one of the mechanisms maintaining these relationships underwent considerable change in the nineteenth century. At the same time new professional occupations developed and some of the older ones were able to consolidate their positions. In the case of the medical profession, which we shall consider in some detail as a paradigm case, the nineteenth century saw both the unification of the profession from three disparate occupational groups, a high-status profession group, the members of a 'craft' and the members of a 'trade', and its consolidation on the basis of more specialised and specific knowledge and responsibilities.

The Emergence of Separate Professions

Whosoever studieth the laws of this realm, who so abideth in the university giving his mind to books, or professeth physic and the liberal sciences, or beside his service in the role of captain of wars or good counsel at home, whereby his commonwealth is benefitted, can live without manual labour, and thereto is able and will bear the post, charge and countenance of a gentleman, he shall for money have a coat and arms bestowed upon him by

16

the heralds (who in the charter of the same do of custom pretend antiquity, service and many gay things) and thereunto being made so good cheap shall be called master, which is the title that men give to esquires and gentlemen, and reputed gentlemen ever after.[3]

This is part of an account of the different orders of British society written by William Harrison in the time of Elizabeth I. It includes the main types of specialised knowledge and task which were compatible with high status in that society. But several of these specialised roles were not rigidly demarcated as separate occupational groups. University teaching, for example, was closely linked to the Church and military service was still for most a part-time activity rather than a full-time career. Specialisation was a less important characteristic of professions than their claim to high status.

One omission from Harrison's list is the Church, but even in the special circumstances of Reformation England, the Church was too extensive and influential an institution to be counted just another profession. The idea of religion as 'the profession' is still held by some members of the Anglican Church.[4] This derives from the ubiquitous role which the Church played in the Middle Ages. At that time the Church controlled access to most types of knowledge and education. Among a largely illiterate population, most of those who could read and write were in some religious orders. The universities were not directly clerical foundations, but most of their members had some links with the Church.[5] Distinction at the university was an accepted route to position in the Church. Theology had pride of place in the curriculum as the 'queen of science', but the medieval universities also provided a practical education for potential statesmen and public servants. Considerable attention was given to training and developing the intellect in abstract, as well as to more specialised subjects, such as law in the European universities and medicine at Oxford as well as in Europe.

The universities drew on two forms of medieval social organisation, the Church and the guild system. As Rashdall points out, the word *universitas* itself refers to the free association of a number of scholars and not specifically to the place at which they worked. In the same way as the guilds, the universities admitted new

17

members to their number by giving them a licence to teach. University degrees gradually became the accepted licence for other forms of professional practice. On the Continent, where Roman law was used in the courts and taught in the universities, the universities were instrumental in creating a large class of professional lawyers. In England a similar association between the legal profession and the universities was prevented by the system of common law, retained and developed in the English courts. Although common law was not considered a proper subject for the universities, the Inns of Court took on some of the functions of a purely legal university in London.[6]

University degrees were not formally required as a necessary qualification for a physician until four years after the establishment of the Royal College in 1518. Nevertheless, before that time the type of medical knowledge used by the physicians was only available at the universities.

The association between the Church and the universities led Rashdall to claim that 'in the north of Europe the church was simply a snyonym for the professions'.[7] Advancement in the professions often involved clerical preferment. Statesmen, public servants and physicians attached to the Royal Court or to particular noblemen might expect to receive a post in the Church as repayment for their services. Gretton has drawn attention to the importance of the development of a monetary economy as a necessary precondition for the emergence of the middle class in general and the professions in particular.[8] Autonomous professional groups were unable to develop while professional services were provided by retainers living within the household of a king or nobleman. Such retainers were dependent on occasional favours from their patron rather than receiving payment for services. Professionals could not gain a livelihood from the receipt of fees until a large enough clientele was available. Even then close association with a few large clients seemed to offer the best chance of occupational and financial security. As we shall see in Chapter 4, this problem is by no means unfamiliar to professionals practising today.

From the time of the Reformation onwards various occupational groups have emerged and separated themselves from the Church. This is one aspect of the general process of the secularisation of society. But in Britain there has been considerable variation

18

in the time and pace at which this process has affected different occupations. The officers and pleaders before the civil law courts benefited from the gradual replacement of the canon law and church courts by the king's justice. The Reformation accelerated this process of separation between Church and State. After the sixteenth century a decreasing number of statesmen and public servants were drawn from the ranks of the clergy. Although the Church was still involved in the licensing of physicians, the formation of the Royal College marks the foundation of a separate occupational group of physicians. Thereafter the main religious influence was that qualifications were denied to non-Anglicans. This was effected through the requirement that physicians should hold a degree from Oxford or Cambridge. But even after the Reformation, the teaching profession at all levels remained closely tied to the Church and largely staffed by clerics.

Parallel to the institutional changes through which separate occupations developed from the Church, there was a gradual change in the type of knowledge applied in professional practice and in the relationship between that knowledge and the religious beliefs of the Church. Although the medieval universities were to some extent institutionally independent, the knowledge available in all subjects was contained within the prevailing religious *Weltanschauung*. Indeed, it could be argued that a distinctive feature of the knowledge taught in universities and necessary for professional practice was that it dealt with areas of life which were important to the religious orthodoxy and areas of potential controversy or conflict. One aspect of what is meant by saying that professions employ a theoretical body of knowledge is that this knowledge includes a set of assumptions, an explicit or implicit theory, about the way the world is and the way society is organised. The development of such knowledge may throw doubt on these basic assumptions. This may in turn threaten other areas of knowledge and by extension the whole structure of society. Although institutional mechanisms may be effective in minimising such threats, there does seem to be a sense in which the traditional professions dealt with areas of life which posed problems both for the organisation of society and for the structure of knowledge within society.

At an institutional level it is interesting to note the coincidence between the development of distinct, secular professions and the

19

introduction of a new body of knowledge separate from the religious orthodoxy. For example, the growth of an independent legal profession is related to the development of common law; the Royal College of Physicians was founded by Thomas Linacre and a few colleagues who rediscovered Greek literature and learning in the medical schools of the Continent; at a later date the secularisation of the teaching profession coincided with change and growth in the curriculum, reflecting the more general expansion of knowledge. In this latter case, however, the process of secularisation was complicated by differences between educational institutions and between those teaching in them. Tropp has pointed out that even after the development of teachers as a secular occupational group, clerical influence was still liable to be found in such institutional machinery as the boards of governors.[9] Nevertheless, we shall see below that the changes and developments which took place in the professions in the nineteenth century were generally accompanied by important changes in the structure of the knowledge which they employed.

Social Status of Pre-Industrial Professions

The professions' responsibilities for areas of life which involved potential social conflict is perhaps a partial reason for their high status. A more specific reason was their association with a high-status clientele drawn from the Royal Court, the aristocracy and the nobility. In the sixteenth century most of the professions were very small, apart from the Church which was itself internally stratified. The Inns of Court and the Royal College of Physicians had memberships numbered in hundreds rather than thousands. But larger occupational groups were also developing alongside the high-status professions. Groups such as the surgeons and the attorneys were eventually able to meet the medical and legal needs of a wider section of society than the small, exclusive professions. Carr-Saunders and Wilson quote a case where a surgeon was accorded as high a status as a physician when both worked for the same royal client.[10] The surgeon and physician who went with Henry V to France in the campaign which led to Agincourt were both given equal recognition and treatment. But the Church did not approve of the shedding of blood, so the surgeons had no

20

contacts with the universities and could not expect ecclesiastical preferment. After an attempt to unite with the physicians in the reign of Henry VI, the surgeons declined in status. In 1540 they united with the barbers, who were recognised only as tradesmen and were organised in a craft guild.

Another important reason why professions were compatible with the social status of gentlemen was that they allowed their members to lead their lives in the style expected of gentlemen. As Harrison put it in the passage quoted above, they were occupations in which a man could live without manual labour and without engaging in commerce or trade. Laslett emphasises the importance of this division in pre-industrial society between those who could call themselves gentlemen and those who had to work for a living.[11] A gentleman was expected to maintain a leisured life-style without actively working to support it. Land, which was the main form of accumulated wealth, was also the basis of the class and status structure. The skill of impoverished young gentlemen in outwitting the demands of tradesmen was a staple ingredient in the plot of man Restoration comedies. The professions fitted into a society in which status was ascribed by family position and inherited wealth by providing the younger sons of the nobility and gentry with a living.

According to Marshall, the characteristic of the professions in pre-industrial society was their compatibility with the 'good life' of gentlemanly leisure.[12] The ideology of professionalism at this time stressed the independence of the professional from employer, client, economic pressure, even from work itself. As Marshall put it, 'the professional man does not work in order to be paid; he is paid in order that he may work'.[13] Indeed, most professional careers involved long periods in which the professional himself paid in order to work. Professional work itself was not sufficiently specialised to be limited to the routine application of a particular expertise to a particular set of problems. The performance of the professional function seems to have been a less important aspect of the professional role than the ability to live a suitably leisured and cultured life. The professional's acquaintance with the knowledge available in society was symbolic of his status position rather than useful as a practical expertise. Indeed, many professionals were able to use their knowledge to follow their own interests in activities quite outside their professional function. Some important

21

contributions to the physical and biological sciences were made by professionals in an amateur capacity.

Other Occupational Groups and the Guild System

This account suggests that professionalism in pre-industrial society was less important as a method of organising work tasks, more important as a means of ensuring status and an appropriate lifestyle. But the division of labour in pre-industrial society also took other forms. The needs of the urban populations in the towns were serviced by skilled tradesmen and craftsmen. Such occupations were more rigorously specialised than the professions, but their members were on the other side of the social gulf between gentlemen and the rest of society.

Ostensibly the difference between these occupations and the professions was one of form – the other occupations involved contact with trade and manual labour. Other differences have already been suggested in explaining why professions were able to claim high status. The nature of the tasks they performed and the clientele they served did not bring these occupations into exclusive contact with the social élite. Nor did they use the body of general or theoretical knowledge available in society which had been mediated through the Church. Unlike most of the high-status professions, these specialised occupations did not offer the individual practitioner any opportunity for outstanding individual success and acclamation. Although success in the professions was often dependent on factors other than effort or ability, such professions as the Bar, the Armed Forces, politics, even the Church, did offer the professional the possibility of unique individual distinction and public recognition.

One of the effects of the guild system in which the trades and crafts were organised was to limit and control competition. In the eleventh century most guilds were societies of merchants formed for their members' economic and physical protection as they traded through Europe. Soon afterwards urban artisans began to unite in similar brotherhoods for protection and mutual aid. But, as Pirenne points out, this process originated not only because the artisans realised the benefits of association, but also because the municipal authorities imposed a structure of control on economic

22

activities in the urban centres.[14] Craft organisation provided a medium through which the authorities could levy taxes and exercise control over production and prices. It also gave the members of the occupation the means to represent their interests to the authorities and to protect themselves from internal and external competition.

Through the guilds the municipal authorities were able to organise the supply of goods and services in the urban economy and to exercise some control over the quality of the product. The guilds were generally controlled by the master craftsmen who formed a small élite at the apex of a regulated career structure. Many guilds were given exclusive rights to engage in particular types of production. Internally they elaborated rules and regulations governing the way this production should be carried on and controlling the hours and conditions of work for their craft.

But tension developed between the guilds and the municipal authorities as the former became more independent and exclusive. In some cases the guilds took over power in the towns and used the structure of economic control to further their own interests. But at the same time a division of interest developed within the guilds between the journeymen and the master craftsmen. The latter controlled the tools of the trade and the raw material and provided work for the journeymen. They also controlled the organisation of the guild and attempted to make their own position exclusive and hereditary by limiting the number of master craftsmen and setting up restrictive entry conditions. This internal conflict between journeymen and masters and the external conflict with the citizens and civic authorities both contributed to the break-up of the system. More important, however, in undermining the position of the guilds were such economic changes as the development of national and international markets. As Pirenne points out, the guilds were suited to the system of regulation adopted in the local economy of the medieval town. They inhibited the growth of a wider economy. They were replaced by capitalist forms of organisation better able to provide the resources for production and distribution on a larger scale.

This brief sketch of the guild system suggests some important parallels between it and later developments among the professions. The guilds were associations of specialised workers; autonomous but integrated into the structure of civil authority; self-governing

23

but usually controlled by a specially recruited élite which on occasions developed into a small, self-perpetuating oligarchy. Each guild supervised training and recruitment for their occupation and exercised some control over performance and practice. The system was based on the assumption that the public interest was best served by ensuring quality production from proved experts. This system of regulated production gave way to *laissez-faire* capitalism in the face of industrial and technical change and an expanding economy. The market mechanism seemed to provide the link between supply and demand necessary to supersede a system of control which had already proved inadequate.

But many, like Durkheim in a passage quoted in Chapter 1, have criticised capitalism for weakness at precisely this point.[15] They have turned to occupational organisation and professional criteria as an alternative method of judging and serving social needs. But this in turn raises the problem of how judgements of need based on professional knowledge and authority are to be linked to public demand and kept within available means. The guild system tended to make the skilled and expert producer rather than the consumer sovereign. This was one of the sources for the ideology of professionalism which emerged during the nineteenth century. It is an aspect of the general problem of containing professional autonomy within the social structure which is one of the continuing themes of this book.

Patronage and Professional Recruitment

By the eighteenth century members of the high-status professions were no longer retainers working within the households of the aristocracy. But there was still a large element of patronage in professional organisation. Many artists, performers and writers were closely associated with individual patrons.[16] These were unable to develop as distinct occupational groups until there was a wider clientele available whom they could reach through such media as the book, the magazine and the newspaper. In many of the traditional high-status professions, including the Church, appointments were in the hands of members of the nobility, gentry or old established institutions such as the universities. This system helped to maintain the link between these groups and the pro-

24

fessions in the status structure. Appointment in a profession provided a niche for the younger sons of the patrons or of their friends. Patronage in government appointments was used to underpin the political system and to gain support for particular factions and parties. Among the more obvious techniques of connection and influence, the purchase system in use in the Army was a curious hybrid. Initially the patronage of a commanding officer was necessary to purchase a commission but once the aspirant was appointed to a regiment, promotion depended upon seniority and the ability to pay for a more expensive position.

Contemporaries justified the purchase system as a means of ensuring the recruitment of officers from the right social backgrounds and of preventing the development of a professional officer élite. Dislike of a professional, full-time standing army as a potential source of conflict in society had been reinforced by the experience of the English revolutionary wars. Reader has pointed out that the only special skill necessary for an army officer at this time was horsemanship, an expertise which was well developed among the country gentry.[17] The other qualities expected of an officer – courage, toughness, a sense of honour, duty and leadership – were also included among the ideal attributes of the country gentry. The purchase system ensured that officers were recruited from this section of society. Only wealthy and established families could be expected to have the necessary means and connections.[18] Moreover, once in the Army, the officer still needed financial support to meet his daily expenses and to secure further promotion. According to Otley, officers in the Home Army were generally unable to live entirely on their army pay until as late as the Second World War.[19]

But the combination of the purchase system with promotion by seniority also prevented the development of personal loyalties and factions within the officer corps. These might have been a problem if appointments had been in the hands of a few aristocrats or patrons. Seniority and promotion were achieved within individual regiments and these did develop as separate foci of loyalty within the Army as a whole. But inter-regimental rivalry, though it might occasionally threaten co-operation and efficiency within the Army, was not likely to provide a basis for divided loyalties in political or social conflict. In the middle of the nineteenth century, when the purchase system and other forms of patronage came under general attack, defenders were quick to claim this as one of its virtues. It avoided some of the dangers of direct patronage and did not involve the injustices of individual favouritism.

Military power is potentially more dangerous to society than power based on other forms of professional authority. Nevertheless, the problem of accommodating the Military within the social structure is a special case of the general problem of reconciling professional autonomy and social organisation.[20] Generally speaking, the chances of conflict between the Army and society can be minimised through arrangements made for recruitment, training or conditions of service. In the eighteenth century army officers were recruited from the families which made up the governing social élite. They retained a similar style of life once appointed. It is interesting to note that specialised institutions for training and socialisation did not develop until the nineteenth century. At the same time recruitment became (slightly) more open, the first specialised officers appeared in the services in engineering and artillery regiments and a new type of full-time career officer emerged in the Indian Army. The organisation of the British Army shows very clearly the contrast between professionalism as a general claim to status and a style of life in society and professionalism based on a full-time, specialised expertise.

Specialisation developed earlier in the Navy than in the Army because as soon as ships stopped being treated simply as floating battlefields specialised skills and expertise became necessary to sail and navigate ships and to use them with the greatest effect in fighting. Elias has documented the conflict between two groups of officers within the British Navy, the 'gentlemen' and the 'tarpaulins'.[21] Pepys coined the dictum that 'among naval officers the seamen were not gentlemen and the gentlemen were not seamen'. The 'gentlemen' were not expected to take part in the manual labour of sailing but were there to command and fight. Apart from a few families which regularly provided naval leaders, they were recruited from the fringes of the same social strata as the army officers and other high-status professions. Younger sons of established families were as likely to join the Navy as the Army or the Church. But the Navy did have a special attraction for those with less secure financial means. It was relatively secure, inexpensive and there was always a chance of large rewards from prize money. The 'tarpaulins', on the other hand, were apprenticed for seven years and trained in the special skills of sailing. The office of 'midshipman', which was not introduced until the eighteenth century, helped to eradicate the division between the two groups by providing a common route of entry. Nevertheless, latent conflict seems to have continued for some time between the high-status amateurs with family connections and the full-time career officers who regarded their fellow officers as such.

Younger sons of the gentry made up most of the recruits in all the high-status professions. The link was particularly clear in the case of the Church. Many livings were in the gift of established families who were able to use them to provide for their dependent members. Political influence or family connections were necessary if a clergyman was to obtain a remunerative position and not to remain an insecure and ill-paid curate. The family might also be expected to provide financial support while the aspirant waited for a living, though university and college offices were another way in which clerical recruits could finance this period of waiting. Financial support to set up a practice was necessary in all the high-status professions. It took some time, for example, for a physician to recruit a clientele, especially as the medicine he practised did not guarantee a cure and was not automatically regarded as essential. Newman has suggested that in spite of the differences in occupational status between the physicians and the surgeons at the beginning of the nineteenth century, the two groups were drawn from much the same social backgrounds.[22] Indeed, he goes further and points out that while there is evidence that a few physicians were drawn from the families of tradesmen and artisans, few surgeons seem to have come from any but upper-middle and professional backgrounds.

Professional Expertise and Professional Education

The processes of recruitment and financial dependence which bound the professions closely to the landed classes were reinforced by the general lack of specialised expertise in any of the high-status professions. In some cases, such as medicine, the state of professional knowledge did not provide much basis for a specialised expertise. The medical skills and learning of a physician were, according to Newman, limited mainly to the art of writing com-

27

plicated prescriptions. He might have extensive learning in classic literature and culture, but he depended on his gentlemanly manner, impressive behaviour and his clients' ignorance to develop a medical practice. In so far as a system of medical education existed at all by the end of the eighteenth century, it depended on the personal initiative of the aspirant to gain his medical knowledge. In London medical knowledge could be obtained either by 'walking the wards' in one of the voluntary hospitals, established in the late eighteenth century, or by attending one of the private schools organised mainly by prominent surgeons working in these hospitals. For those with the necessary resources, a trip to Edinburgh or the Continent was also useful. Such medical education, however, played little part in helping the candidate to meet the requirements of the licensing authorities. The Royal Colleges had allowed their educational activities to lapse and the examinations which they conducted made little pretence at testing medical knowledge.

The Royal Colleges were two of the most important licensing bodies in an extremely complex and varied licensing system. The fact that responsibility for licensing did not involve any responsibility for education emphasises that there was little relationship between professional training and professional status at this stage in the development of professionalism. In so far as the examinations had a function, it was to ensure that the candidates had the latent status characteristics commensurate with their claim to be accepted into an exclusive professional body. The modern concept of an examination as a test only becomes relevant in the nineteenth century, first as a more rational test of latent status characteristics and later, in other occupations, as a test of technical competence. Some changes in the content of professional training and the system of professional recruitment parallel the development of professions as specialised occupations responsible for the performance of specific tasks, based on expert knowledge. This general process of development, which is the subject of this chapter, also involved important changes in the structure and function of the education system and in the content of the educational experience. These changes have posed problems which are still not entirely resolved within the education system and in its relationship to the occupational structure. But such continuing ambiguities and controversies serve to emphasise the importance of an historical perspective to any understanding of contemporary social institutions.

Most of the graduates of Oxford and Cambridge, the two institutions at the apex of the loosely-organised and unextensive system of education operating prior to the nineteenth century, went into the Church.[23] They were not expected to be specially qualified in theology but to have a general acquaintance with classical learning. But at this time the universities were far from providing an effective education in any field. Armytage quotes the indictment of Bishop Burnett who claimed that 'in the universities they [ordinands] for most part lost the learning they brought with them from schools and learned so very little in them that too commonly they came from them less knowing than when they went to them'.[24] Nevertheless, even literacy was still at a premium in society at that time and some of the livings in the poorest parishes, for which there was no demand, had to be filled by men with no better qualification than that they could read and write. Laslett has pointed to the more diffuse functions of the clergy as sources of information and leaders of opinion in a rural society in which most of the population was illiterate and which had few other communication media.[25] In Halevy's phrase, the clergy were able to 'enhance the moral influence of their cloth by the social influence of their rank'.[26]

But the legal profession in the eighteenth century provides the most remarkable example of a high-status profession lacking specialised training and expertise, if only because of the contrast with the situation at the end of the sixteenth century. Up to that time the Inns of Court had been active educational institutions. Lectures, disputations and 'moots' or mock law suits were all part of a system of education which drew on the medieval traditions of oral disputation. The 'moots' in particular involved all the members of the Inn and must have played an important part in cementing the occupational group as well as giving students practical training. But by the middle of the eighteenth century 'at the Middle Temple all the obligations of the student could be compounded for £38 6s 2d, this being the total sum due in fines where a gentleman forfeits his vocations, keeps not his terms and fails in the performance of his exercises'.[27]

The system of vocational training seems to have finally disappeared in the period of Cromwell's government. All that remained were financial provisions, such as those quoted above, and the requirement that students should attend the Inns if only to eat dinners. Among a group as small as the barristers this provision does not seem to be without importance in encouraging professional solidarity.[28]

In the other professions, entry procedures had become just as much a matter of routine formalities. In the Church the bishop was expected to know personally or by repute that each candidate was 'a man of virtuous conversation and without crime'. The more rigorous requirements that a man should have a knowledge of Latin and of the Scriptures could be waived if the candidate was known to be a gentleman. The other qualifications served only as symbols of this status. Examinations for the Licentiate and the Fellowship of the Royal College of Physicians were brief, oral, conducted in Latin and covered the classical languages and a few fields of medicine. The important qualification was a degree from Oxford or Cambridge. This was even preferred to a degree from a Continental or Scottish university, though by the end of the eighteenth century these were giving vocational medical education in the newly developed areas of medical science. Graduates of these universities were unable to become more than licentiates of the Royal College unless they also held an English qualification. There was little or no instruction in any subject at this time at Oxford or Cambridge, and especially none in medicine.

But no matter how vague the educational requirements or how much of a formality the recruitment procedures, the leaders of all the professions justified their systems on the grounds that they ensured that only men of the necessary social standing gained access to the professions. As early as 1425 the gubernator of Lincoln's Inn can be found claiming the expense of legal education as a virtue because it ensured that 'the students are sons of persons of quality, those of inferior rank not being able to bear the expense'.[29] But the waves of criticism against educational procedures which developed in the nineteenth century, both within and outside the professions, produced some of the most explicit defences of their status functions. Church leaders faced with a fall in recruitment in the second half of the nineteenth century resisted attempts to lower entry qualifications and to break the connection with the universities on the grounds that this would threaten the clergy's social position. For example, a speaker at the Church Congress of 1872 claimed that 'owing to the union of the character

30

of the clergyman with the social status of gentleman, in fitting him for the latter, they [the universities] have in a manner fitted him for the former. . . .'[30] Leaders of the Royal College of Physicians used similar arguments to defend their position in public before such bodies as the Select Committee of 1833, as well as internally against the other branches of the medical profession and their own licentiates. As we saw above, even the purchase system in the Army did not lack supporting argument.

Nevertheless, law and medicine stand out as two professions in which some skill seems to be a prerequisite for practice even at a time when specialised knowledge was extremely limited. Reader makes the point that, though in both cases the aspirant was admitted to a small group of social equals on the basis of diffuse status criteria, 'the incompetent, the unlucky and the under-financed were shaken out after admission' in the competitive process of finding clients and establishing a practice.[31] Sir Henry Acland, a physician at the beginning of the nineteenth century, advised a contemporary to 'send the boy to Oxford and let him pay there no attention to his future profession, but do as he would if he were going to parliament like you. When he has taken his degree, send him to me and I will tell him what next.'[32] Various channels were open to the aspirant or the newly qualified professional through which he personally could learn the skills of his occupation and acquire some experience of working in it.

But throughout this period the other group of occupations which were later recognised as professions were more specialised in their skills and tasks, used different training and recruitment procedures and were regarded as of lower status than the professions discussed so far. The most important of these were the lower-status branches of the legal and medical professions, the attorneys and the surgeons and apothecaries. All practised much more widely among the population than the high-status professions. In the legal profession public access was one of the differences between the barristers, who were pleaders before the courts, and the attorneys, who acted more generally as agents for their clients. The apothecaries won the right to prescribe as well as to make up medicines through a court case because of the demand for advice as well as drugs from potential patients. As demand for legal and medical services increased, these groups were the first to feel the benefit. The attorneys, for example, were able to base

31

secure practices on the legal work associated with land ownership and transfer. Their work was increased by the changes in the systems of agriculture, industry and transport which occurred in the eighteenth century and which created many disputes over land use and title.[33]

Guild organisation survived in the medical occupations in such forms as the Company of Surgeons and the Society of Apothecaries. These bodies controlled their occupational groups, laid down regulations for training and apprenticeship and set qualifications for membership. However, their powers to control the misappropriation of their name or the usurpation of their functions were not extensive. Although apprenticeship suggested some form of practical training and experience, supervision was loose and experience might be no more than that of a poorly paid and menial assistant. The examinations conducted by the two bodies had little stringency until changes were made at the beginning of the nineteenth century.

The Change from Status to Occupational Professions: The Case of Medical Practice

The various changes which occurred in the professions and in the ideology of professionalism during the nineteenth century can all be linked to the basic change outlined at the beginning of this chapter, in the importance of occupation within the economic and social structure. From being a hindrance to any claims to social status, occupation has become a key indicator of social position. In pre-industrial society the status professions were able to maintain a foothold among the ranks of the gentlemen by glossing over their work responsibilities and emphasising the leisured and honourable life-style which their members could adopt. Professional learning was not a specific and useful expertise so much as an acquaintance with a culture which had an accepted value in society, if no obvious vocational relevance. The status professions were each loosely responsible for a particular problem area in society, but their responsibilities were ill-defined, not spread throughout the community and inadequately backed by knowledge and expertise.

Change in the structure of the medical profession in the first

32

half of the nineteenth century provides a useful example through which to examine the transformation of this type of professionalism into modern, occupational professionalism.[34] A unified medical profession gradually emerged from the combination of a status profession, the physicians, with two less prestigious occupational groups, the surgeons and the apothecaries. The medical profession is especially useful as a paradigm because the various traditions of professional and occupational organisation, discussed earlier in this chapter, came to be combined within the same occupational group. It illustrates the historical continuity in the midst of social change, which makes the historical perspective sketched in this chapter necessary to an understanding of modern professions and professionalism. The medical case is also specially relevant because the medical profession is often held to represent the professional ideal in modern society. It ranks high in social prestige and financial remuneration and it performs essential services within the community backed by specialised and effective knowledge and expertise. But although the medical profession serves as a useful illustration of this general process of change, the process took different forms in other occupations. Some of these will be considered later in this chapter.

The division between the three types of medical practitioner, the physician, surgeon and apothecary, covered differences in function, organisation and social standing. Ostensibly there was a division of labour between the three groups. The physicians were responsible for internal medicine, the surgeons for external treatment and the apothecaries for the prescription of drugs. Throughout the eighteenth century this formal division of responsibility had increasingly little relevance to medical practice, especially outside London. The apothecaries in particular fought a series of battles with the physicians over their right to give medical advice as well as to prescribe drugs. The Great Plague of 1665 gave unexpected encouragement to their cause. Most physicians left London for the relative safety of the country, leaving the apothecaries with a clear field in which to practise. Early in the eighteenth century the apothecaries' right to charge for their services was challenged in the courts. The decision of the trial court was reversed on appeal to the House of Lords. Their lordships found that the apothecary William Rose was entitled to charge for the drugs he prescribed, though not for his advice. This secured the

33

apothecaries' financial position, though a latent consequence may well have been to give the prescription of drugs a central place in medical treatment. It was not until after the passage of the Apothecaries Act of 1815 that another court case allowed apothecaries the right to charge simply for advice. While the apothecaries were establishing their position, the physicians engaged in various activities designed to irritate or frustrate the ambitions of their junior colleagues. In particular the right of the Royal College of Physicians to search the premises of apothecaries in London for 'bad drugs' was strengthened in 1723. This became an issue in the controversy between the two groups. The apothecaries feared, apparently with justification, that the physicians might misuse their power of search.

The physicians themselves sought to maintain their position as the acknowledged leaders in the medical field, claiming the full status of cultivated gentlemen. Carr-Saunders and Wilson suggest that the scientific enterprise and learning of many sixteenth-century physicians was replaced by a moribund preoccupation with the forms of cultured gentility. The novelty of the scientific revolution had worn off by the eighteenth century.[35] Certainly by the beginning of the nineteenth century defenders of the physicians' position as a privileged caste were prepared to argue simply in terms of their social standing. As one witness to the Select Committee on Medical Education of 1834 put it, classical learning and general cultivation of the mind were necessary if the physician was not to be found at a loss in the great houses of the land which it was his duty to enter. 'The select group of English physicians' have been summed up by Holloway as '. . . trained to be first and foremost gentlemen. They were familiar with the writings of Greek and Latin scholars; their medical knowledge was acquired in libraries rather than by contact with the sick. Even when they came to practise they rarely saw any patients.'[36]

In the second half of the eighteenth century the exclusive group of fellows of the Royal College of Physicians – they numbered as few as 113 even in 1834[37] – were continually attacked by the junior licentiates who were excluded from exercising any say in the college's affairs. Many of these were barred from full membership of the college as they lacked the qualification of a degree from Oxford or Cambridge. No matter that virtually no medicine was included in the degree requirements of either university. The

34

fellows of the college were still prepared to defend the qualification on the grounds that it was essential to the survival of the universities as well as to the standing of the physicians. The licentiates, on the other hand, increasingly possessed Scottish or Continental degrees which did include some medical education and they were generally drawn from similar social backgrounds to the fellows who despised them. The licentiates continually challenged the legality of the restrictive regulations which governed the college but they were only successful in winning token concessions. The governing body regarded their pressure as coming from people of low birth, bad education and a 'democratical and levelling spirit'. Underlying the internal controversy between the two grades in the college were wider social questions about the methods and extent to which medicine should be provided for the whole population of the country. Similar arguments occur in the clashes between the physicians and the apothecaries.

The surgeons' guild was also riven by similar internal conflicts. The surgeons separated themselves from the barbers' company in 1745. Through continued organisational ineptitude the court of the new company found itself in a situation at the end of the century when it was advised that its own constitution and authority was not legal. The court had allowed the teaching and examining functions of the company, never very extensive, to run down. Shortly before attempting to reorganise and ratify its own position, it had sold off the company's hall. The members managed to mobilise sufficient opposition to stop two Bills embodying the reorganisation plans passing parliament only to have the changes imposed by Royal Charter. In this somewhat ignominious fashion the surgeons acquired their own Royal College on 22 March 1800. As Holt-Smith points out, both these disputes within the Royal College of Physicians and the Company of Surgeons can be seen as similar to the controversies over leadership which developed in most guilds as the guild system itself declined.[38]

But outside the medical guilds themselves, important changes were developing in the science of medicine and the clientele whom it served. Together these two factors played a crucial part in changing the nature of the medical occupation and its claim to social standing in the way outlined earlier in this chapter. The development of scientific medical studies in anatomy and physiology spread from Continental medical centres to Scotland and eventually to England. It was inhibited in England by the power of the two Royal Colleges, by the lack of any centres for formal medical education and by suspicious social attitudes towards medical science in general, reflected, for example, in the law prohibiting the use of human bodies for research.

Population growth, industrial change and urban development also radically altered the structure of society in which medicine was to be practised. While the physicians still thought in terms of service to the nobility and gentry with some charitable provision for their servants, the apothecaries and to a lesser extent the surgeons were increasingly called on to make provision for the urban, industrial middle class as well as the urban poor. Much of the controversy between the apothecaries and the physicians centred on the fomer's claim to be better able to meet the needs of this new clientele. In spite of some token attempts by the physicians to provide clinics, they were too few in number, especially in the provinces, to challenge the apothecaries and the jointly qualified surgeon-apothecaries. In the early nineteenth century the term 'general practitioner' came into use to refer to this type of doctor, practising more widely in the community.

Carr-Saunders and Wilson go so far as to argue that it was the increased medical activity of the apothecaries which produced the improvement in public health at the end of the eighteenth century.[39] Changes in medical science were slow, however, in giving doctors the means to combat disease effectively. Holloway emphasises the weak position of the eighteenth-century medical professional in relation to his client.[40] He had little guarantee that his claims to professional knowledge would be borne out by any improvement in the patient's condition. Instead there seems to have been a tendency to rely on convincing the client of the efficacy of various universal nostra or panaceas. The public seem to have remained largely unconvinced of claims to professional expertise, however, though they were impressed by medical division and disorder. Vaughan quotes the comments printed in the Annual Register of 1832 following an epidemic in that year. Such epidemics were all too common at the time. 'The cholera left medical men as it found them – confirmed in most opposite opinions, or in total ignorance as to its nature, its cure and the cause of its origin, if endemic – or the mode of transmission, if it were infectious.'[41] The weak position of practitioners in relation

36

to public authorities as well as individual clients was graphically demonstrated when the Poor Law Amendment Act of 1834 instituted local economies in poor relief. These drastically cut medical provision for those on relief. The architect of the Act and of the machinery which it set up, Edwin Chadwick, was outspoken in preferring preventive public health medicine to the uncertainties of curative medicine, founded on the need for professional employment.

The Society of Apothecaries was the first medical corporation to take seriously its responsibilities for professional training and so to make a move towards linking licensing and education. The apothecaries desired to ratify their advance in status from tradesmen to medical practitioners. The Apothecaries Act of 1815 was the result of several attempts to pass legislation reorganising their branch of the profession. The Act did not achieve all for which its sponsors had hoped. In the face of opposition from the two Royal Colleges and from the chemists and druggists who had taken over the apothecaries' places as medical shopkeepers, provisions to prohibit practice by the uneducated and to set up a medical school were dropped. The Act gave the Society power to supervise apprenticeship, examine apothecaries and license practice throughout England and Wales. The apothecary's right to recover fees was written into the Act, thus providing a small inducement to encourage apothecaries to seek recognition by the Society, but in practice there was little force behind the licensing provisions. Unqualified and uneducated practitioners were able to continue in practice largely unhindered. The Act began the process which was continued more rigorously in later Acts of discouraging unqualified practice by hedging it with disadvantages rather than by attempting to ban it directly.

The Society wasted no time after the passage of the Act in working out a system of examinations and educational requirements which would ensure that future licentiates of the society had some medical knowledge. As well as requiring a period of apprenticeship, the Society also demanded evidence of attendance at lectures, which it organised, and of experience in hospitals. The fact that the first move towards examining professional competence should have come from the least prestigious branch of the profession is an indication of the developing importance of professional expertise as the basis of professional status. The L.S.A.

37

became an increasingly popular qualification during the first half of the nineteenth century. Many took the trouble to combine it with a qualification in surgery. In a time of disorder in medicine generally, when quackery was rife, practitioners were beginning to seek security in such formalised knowledge as was available.

The first half of the nineteenth century also saw the first moves towards occupational organisation in the medical profession. The British Medical Association traces its origins to the Provincial Medical and Surgical Association founded by a group of provincial doctors in Worcester in 1832. While the medical corporations were centred on the metropolis and controlled by exclusive oligarchies, the P.M.S.A. was avowedly provincial, an association with the twin aims of providing provincial arenas for study and debate and of representing and advancing the interests of the new-style provincial general practitioner. The P.M.S.A. was soon involved in fighting for the status and remuneration of doctors employed by the new Poor Law Guardians established under the Act of 1834. It developed contact with the Government and parliament and brought pressure to bear on other issues such as the Act of 1836 requiring registration of births and deaths. This side of its work, as well as the need to represent the whole profession, eventually required the Association to move to headquarters in London and to change its title to the B.M.A.

Another step towards occupational development was the foundation of the 'Lancet' in 1824 as a journal of medical knowledge and opinion. The 'Lancet' was the creation of Thomas Wakley, a medical reformer and campaigner, who played a prominent part in the legislative attempts to unify and rationalise the structure of the profession in the middle of the century. The path to the Medical Act of 1858 was strewn with defeated Bills and the reports of two select committees – one on medical education in 1934 and the other on Medical Registration in 1847. The first committee gave the reformers a public platform through which to attack the state on medical education and examination. The second exposed the prevalence of unlicensed and unqualified practice which impeded the growth of order and unity in the occupation. But the demand for a radical reorganisation of the education system, the examination system and the structure of the profession according to the principles of rational utilitarianism, were blocked by the opposing interests of the established authorities.

38

The Act of 1858 was a compromise which brought unity to the profession by recognising its disorder. All the licensing and educational bodies then in existence were recognised, but they were put under the overall supervision of a newly created General Medical Council. This body, made up of nominees of the Crown, the medical corporations, the universities and later from the profession at large, was made responsible to the Privy Council for maintaining a central register of medical practitioners. Practitioners were to be admitted to the register through the existing educational and examining bodies. Further progress towards unity and rationalisation was slow. The G.M.C.'s powers to control these bodies were very limited and in the years following the Act it used its influence sparingly. However, considerable spontaneous improvement had already taken place in educational facilities, especially in London where medical schools developed around the voluntary hospitals, often drawing on the resources of the earlier private schools. The first such school developed from the foundation of University College, London, in 1827. In this way the schools were linked to both the hospitals and the university. The G.M.C. was also given power to discipline practitioners by striking them off the register. Responsibility for discipline, which in a sense meant representing the interests of the community as well as the profession, was thus not given directly to the colleague group but to an administrative body which did not include direct professional representation until some time later.

Although the Medical Act of 1858 is generally taken as marking the foundation of a single unified medical profession, there is a real sense in which its importance rests more on hindsight and the need for historical landmarks than on the immediate achievements of the Act. Nevertheless, the general course of change within the medical profession was clear by this time. A single regulatory body had been established embracing the old guild organisations and standing between the profession and the community and the State. The old organisations retained considerable power and the development of medical knowledge and professional education gave more content to their responsibilities. The system of licensing was used to assess expert knowledge and ability, not simply to ratify membership of a status group. The increase in urban population provided new demands for medical services, at the same time as advances in medical knowledge began to give doctors some means

39

of meeting them. The occupation showed some collective awareness of its common identity and interests by setting up channels of
internal communication and association.

Change in Other Professions

Like the medical profession, the legal profession at the beginning
of the nineteenth century was internally divided and stratified.[42]
Again it was the lower branch of the profession, the attorneys and
solicitors, who first showed interest in occupational organisation
and professional education. Cultivation of unity within the occupation and the development of a professional expertise seem to be
two ways in which professionals whose status was not already
sanctified by gentlemanly connections sought to improve their
authority and social position. Attorneys and solicitors were
sufficiently mistrusted by society in the eighteenth century to
attract a number of regulating Acts of Parliament. These included
one in 1729 which instituted a regular system of articled training.
The first 'Law Society', actually titled 'The Society of Gentleman
Practisers in the Courts of Law and Equity', was founded shortly
afterwards and flourished throughout the rest of the century. The
society attempted to develop standard procedures for training and
qualification, to supervise professional practice and to improve its
quality, and to represent the interests of the attorneys in relation
to the Bar and society in general. The development of occupational self-consciousness seems to have been at least in part a
response to external intervention as embodied in the Act of 1729
and public criticism of the attorneys at this time. This factor of
external intervention and influence has a continual, if paradoxical,
importance in fostering professional autonomy. The connections
between this first 'Law Society' and 'The Society of Attorneys,
Solicitors, Proctors and others not being Barristers, practising in
the Courts of Law and Equity in the United Kingdom', founded
in 1825, are obscure. This second body is the direct antecedent of
the modern 'Law Society'. It began to take responsibility for
educational provision by instituting lecture courses and taking
part with the judges in establishing written examinations.

The Inns of Court, on the other hand, which controlled the
senior branch of the profession, showed little interest in changing

the perfunctory formalities which led to a call to the Bar for more rigorous tests of legal knowledge. Legal knowledge was not taught at the Inns or at the old universities. It was not until the foundation of University and King's Colleges in London that academic legal instruction became available. The Inns did bow to pressure from a Select Committee in 1846 and a Royal Commission in 1854 and established some teaching posts and a course of lectures. Some examinations were also instituted but they were not made compulsory until 1872. The Inns argued that the intense competition to build a practice in the courts after the call to the Bar was a sufficient test of competence. In sociological terms we might speculate that this, together with the cost and difficulty of qualifying in the Inns, was a better technique for selecting according to latent status characteristics than any attempts to test for manifest professional skills.

The development of scientific medical knowledge seems to have been of crucial importance in providing the doctors with a universal professional expertise. Other professions had greater difficulty in specifying a body of knowledge or expertise which would form a universal basis for professional practice and which could be taught as such to aspiring professionals. In an earlier section we noted that the academic study of law in England was hampered by the use of common rather than Roman law. Only the Church and the physicians maintained contact with the older universities throughout the seventeenth and eighteenth centuries when they were in decline as educational institutions. Various types of apprenticeship, articling or pupillage were the most widespread forms of professional education in the lower-status, occupational professions. These reflected the local, empirical nature of professional practice rather than the universality of its skills. In architecture the movement towards education and examination which developed in the second half of the nineteenth century, sponsored by the Royal Institute of British Architects, had to contend with the counter argument that architecture was an individual art which could not be turned into a routine professional skill.[43] The relationship between individual creativity and professional routinisation is a complex one to which we shall return in Chapter 4. But it is interesting to note, as Kaye points out, that this period of professionalisation within architecture coincided with a period of routinisation in architectural style

Most of the technical and service professions which developed through the nineteenth century as a direct or indirect consequence of the Industrial Revolution followed the same pattern as the architects, depending initially on education through apprenticeship, coupled later with a system of examination and qualification for professional membership organised by the professional association itself. Systems of vocational and professional education were established outside the formal system of higher education. In making their own arrangements for education and examination, becoming 'qualifying associations' in Millerson's terms,[44] such associations were apparently following the example of the medical and legal guilds in the older professions. But the status professions had some links with the older universities or at least with the style of life and culture which they purveyed. Attendance at university, acquaintance with that culture and membership of such a profession were all claims to social prestige. Developments in the 'qualifying associations', however, were strongly vocational.

So too were the few new links which were forged between new professions and such new institutions in the system of higher education as London University. The process was begun in University College, London, which early in its existence began to teach both medicine and law. A chair of engineering had also been planned at University College. King's College, its rival, managed to establish a department before the plan at University College was realised. Gradually the older universities also began to make room for more technical and vocational subjects, but the process of integration was slow. The universities regarded such new subjects with suspicion and their attitude was matched by doubts within the professions about the need for formalised education and about the relevance of academic learning to professional practice. Halsey has pointed to the contrast between even the limited vocationalism of the Victorian civic universities and both the Oxbridge tradition which preceded them and the ideology of some of the new foundations which have followed them in our own time.[45]

In the period of utilitarian reform in the 1830s and 1840s the Church came under attack along with other established institutions. Membership of the established Church was still an essential qualification for many social positions. The dissenters who were excluded from many offices by such provisions sought to limit the Church's prerogatives at the same time as others began to question the value of a Church whose ministers were often not trained in theology or divinity. Within the Church these attacks brought such responses as the Evangelical Movement and the contrasting High Church, Oxford Movement. These were both attempts to redefine the Church's and so by implication the clergy's role in society. Both drew, in rather different ways, on the central expertise of the Church in theological matters. They both played a part in the theological college movement in the middle of the century. This led to the foundation of a number of colleges in which aspirants to the ministry were to be exposed to clerical knowledge and expertise in a way which was hardly attempted at Oxford or Cambridge. But although bishops began to show interest in testing the theological knowledge of those they ordained, there was still plenty of scope for entering the Church on the old terms as a cultivated gentleman. Success in a classical course at an older university was a better qualification for clerical appointment than success in straight theology. Halevy suggests that at the end of the century the old-style country parson, linked to the rural squirearchy, had been joined by another type of clergyman who might be more ardent in the performance of his religious duties, but who did not share the former's social status.[46] The difference between these two types seems to be essentially similar to the divisions which we have already discussed within the medical and legal professions, though in the case of the Church the pattern of stratification was not formally institutionalised. Thus although professionalisation in modern society is usually discussed as a process of raising the status of an occupation and its practitioners, the development of professionalism in the nineteenth century had paradoxically ambiguous consequences for the status of different types of practitioner. This ambiguity resulted from a meeting between the old tradition of status professionalism and the new tendency towards occupational specialisation.

Professional Education, Examinations and the Education System

The nineteenth century saw the beginning of various experiments with different systems of occupational selection and training and of debate about their vocational and social consequences. Such

43

issues are still important and relevant to the sociological study of professional training which has gained momentum in recent years and which is discussed in Chapter 3. Utilitarian pressure for reform in the structure of the professions in the first half of the nineteenth century focused attention on their ability to perform the social functions which they claimed as theirs. Procedures for selection, training and recruitment were not rationally organised to maximise professional expertise. One response to this attack on the loose system of status recruitment was the development of single-purpose professional training schools. These appeared first in the Church, and later in teaching and the Army. The development of such schools seems to have been a product both of the threat to established recruitment procedures which might alter the social composition of the group and of the need to develop and accommodate a more specific occupational expertise within the profession.

Such schools attempted, however uncertainly, to define and pass on a central core of professional knowledge and skill. But more than that, such schools held themselves responsible for selecting aspirants who had the latent status characteristics desired for the profession, and further they tried to develop such characteristics as the trainees passed through the schools. The theological colleges, the military academies and the normal schools or teachers' training colleges all had a wider conception of their function than simply imparting academic knowledge or practical skill. The normal schools were to play an important part in developing a separate profession of teaching and establishing its social position in society. Unlike the professional schools in the other two professions, they were not resisting a threat to a profession and recruitment system already established. But all these single-profession training schools tried to ensure that their graduates fitted their conception of a professional man in their field. In a case such as the Church, where different colleges were founded by different sections within the whole organisation, such as the High Church group and the Evangelicals, colleges might be found aiming at different conceptions of the ministerial role.

Other changes occurred in the recruitment system of the Army. New examination systems were established to select candidates for entry. The idea of written examinations was a new development, peculiar to the first half of the nineteenth century. The aim was

44

to replace such old techniques as oral disputation, which had fallen into disuse and disrepute, with a more efficient, independent and tangible method of judging between candidates. They were introduced into the requirements for a degree at the older universities and became a symbol for the reform movement in their attack on privilege, aristocratic connection and the irrationality of traditional methods of recruitment and professional organisation. Examinations to test general competence were to replace the various systems of patronage which had operated in such fields as the Army and government service.

In the Army formal education, professional training and examination developed first in the more practical and lower status regiments such as the Artillery and the Engineers. The Army's poor performance in the Crimean War served as a stimulus for internal reorganisation and external criticism. In particular the purchase system and the traditional dominance of the officer corps by the landed gentry and the aristocracy came under attack. There were clearly necessary skills and a body of knowledge to be acquired by artillery or engineer officers. But the switch from purchase to examination as the general system of recruitment for non-technical regiments is an important indication of the latent as well as the manifest functions of the new system. Sir Charles Trevelyan who campaigned for 'open' competitive recruitment by examination in a variety of occupations commented in 1867 : '. . . when, by the abolition of purchase and the increase of pay, the army shall become an open, remunerative profession, it will be an object of desire for the best class of our young men who now enter the artillery and engineers, the Indian Civil Service, the law, the civil engineers or any other line of life'.[47] The campaign which eventually resulted in the abolition of purchase in 1871 was aimed primarily at opening another area of occupational opportunity to the sons of the new middle class.

By itself the abolition of purchase was not sufficient to achieve such an aim. The Army was comparatively slow in acquiring the new characteristics of the occupational profession, one of which was that it should provide sufficient remuneration to support the practitioner in his chosen career.[48] Studies of selection and recruitment to high rank in the Army have shown the durability of the aristocratic connection and the slow increase in the numbers from middle-class backgrounds.[49] The Indian Army was to some extent

45

exceptional. Service in it had many disadvantages compared with service in the Home Army. A posting in the Indian Army involved long tours of unglamorous duty away from the centres of power and influence in England. There were also continuous military duties to be performed in frontier campaigns, border patrols or supporting the internal administration. Again this fits the pattern suggested for other occupations. The lower-status branch of the profession was more involved in the performance of professional tasks and also more likely to be recruited from those with lower-status backgrounds.

Sir Charles Trevelyan, as well as arguing that a career in the Army should be open to those with talent, was also careful to note that recruitment by examination would probably encourage rather than hamper selection from aristocratic families. 'Our aristocratic families are so impressed with the necessity of giving their sons the best possible education . . . that we need be under no apprehension about their obtaining their fair share in this as well as every other profession. . . . Whatever raises the standard of education in a profession gives an advantage to the upper class.'[50] Although allowance must be made for the fact that this was a tactical argument directed at the potential opponents of Trevelyan's campaign, it serves to reinforce the point that the system of selection by examination was important as a mechanism of social recruitment. It widened but did not basically subvert the structure of recruitment as it had been under the system of direct patronage. Moreover, in other occupations as well as the Army transition between the two systems was slow and gradual.

Trevelyan was part author of the celebrated Northcote–Trevelyan Report published in 1854 on 'The Organisation of the Permanent Civil Service'. This advocated a system of open competition for recruitment to the Home Civil Service such as had already been introduced for the Civil Service in India by an Act of the previous year.[51] It proved easier to institute such a system in India than in England, where rights and privileges of long-standing were threatened by any move towards change. Although the Civil Service Commission was established a year after the publication of the report, initially it made only slow progress towards the goal of open competition for appointments. The first competitive systems consisted of several separate competitions for different appointments. These were eventually incorporated into a single competition for most departments, although the Foreign Office and the diplomatic corps continued to reserve the right to make their own arrangements. The competitions, before and after consolidation, were designed as a general test of ability and quality. The aim was to pick the best men available on the assumption that their general ability would enable them to do any specific job in the Civil Service, helped of course by experience obtained from actually working in the service. Kelsall in his study of the higher Civil Service quotes two dictums attributed to Harold Laski, which sum up the beliefs which the Civil Service developed from this system. First, there was the assumption that truth would always be revealed by discussion; secondly, a complete confidence that those judged sufficiently able or excellent for appointment would be able to solve and understand any problem.[52]

Some of the reformers had campaigned for examinations as a more specific test of vocational preparation. In other occupations, those we have termed occupational professions, the lack of necessary professional knowledge among recruits was a more important impetus towards the introduction of training and examination. The examinations instituted by the qualifying associations were almost universally attempts to test professional knowledge and improve vocational preparation. Thus although there was a similar movement towards the introduction of examinations in both cases, conceptually there were two different recruitment systems, differing in their origins, aims and consequences.

One important consequence of the system of open competition developed in the Indian and Home Civil Service was that it provided support for the established system of higher education at a time when this appeared to have lost purpose and function. The ability which was measured by the competitive examinations was largely the ability to acquire the range of knowledge and learning covered by the educational institutions. Prominent among the subjects examined, even for entry to the Royal Military Academy at Woolwich for training as an artillery officer, were English language and history and classical languages, literature and history. In a concession to vocationalism, mathematic abilities were prized highly at Woolwich, though they featured in other competitive systems devised for the civil services. They had also been part of the traditional university curriculum, set up in the Middle

Ages. The natural sciences and developing technical disciplines such as civil or mechanical engineering, which had not yet found their way into any but the new university in London, were hardly covered by the examination systems. The virtues of classical learning have been extolled in terms almost identical to those used to advocate the virtues of a competitive system testing general ability. Study of the classics was held to cultivate mental properties and attitudes which would fit the student to handle any subsequent situation. Such claims were self-justifying because of the central role given to classical knowledge in the new examination systems.

There was other historical support for the belief that classical learning was a mark of general quality and ability. As we saw in a previous section, the physicians had used it to support their claim to gentlemanly status and superiority within medicine. Neither occupation nor education then possessed their modern significance as marks of social status, but classical learning was an important symbol, especially for those in more marginal positions in the ascriptive hierarchy. Armytage in his study of university development quotes a comment from Prebendary Gaisford of Durham who was in no doubt about the advantages of such an education.[53] Classical education 'enables us to look down with contempt on those who have not shared its advantages, and also fits us for places of emolument in this world and the next'. But whether or not classical education was as effective as its proponents claimed in cultivating general habits of mind, it certainly played an important part in training the governing class of late Victorian England and in giving it a common ideology.

This common ideology, as expounded, for example, by Wilkinson, owes much to the tradition of gentlemanly behaviour and status discussed earlier in this chapter.[54] A new element was the ideal of public service and the idea of public trust vested in those who were fortunate enough to have had opportunities of birth and education. But other elements such as the concept of leisure for work rather than work for leisure, the preference for amateurism rather than expertness and the generalised ideal of a cultured, literate gentleman were more directly derivative from the older tradition. The importance of this ideology and style in life is graphically demonstrated by the part it played in giving colonial adminstrators, for example, a core of common behaviour and culture closely linked to the home country. The conflicting claims

48

of experts and amateurs in government are still argued out. The contrasting claims are both linked to the development of professionalism, each drawing on a different tradition within it.[55]

Wilkinson, following Weber, draws a parallel between the education systems of Imperial China and Imperial Britain. In both cases the syllabus concentrated on a formal system of knowledge, empty of practical content, and in both cases similar ideologies of public service and cultivated behaviour developed among the governing class. Weber had also drawn attention to the existence of two different educational ideals in different social systems.[56] In one case education functioned as a ratification of status and the educational ideal was a liberal, generally educated, cultured man. In the other, education was intended to provide specific training and expertise to equip people for the performance of particular social tasks.

It is a peculiar irony of educational development that this 'liberal', classical form of education which seemed inherently non-vocational was made the basis for a vocational, educational system. The non-vocational content was turned into a means of vocational preferment by the form adopted for the competitive systems in the civil and military services, by the prestige accorded to classical education in some of the more traditional professions, such as the Church, and by its general acceptance as a symbol of status and ability. The introduction of competitive examinations, designed to 'open' recruitment into élite positions, had the effect of formalising and institutionalising the connection between the occupational élites and the social élites. Traditionally prestigious areas of knowledge were used as the content of the system and access to this knowledge was limited, through the hierarchy of educational institutions.

At the basis of the educational system were the public schools. Existing schools went through considerable reorganisation in the first half of the century. New forms of organisation and educational philosophies were hammered out by such headmasters as Arnold at Rugby. Many more schools were founded in the second half of the century, often with specific aims to train boys for clerical, professional, military or colonial service and to make educational provision for the sons of such professionals. Wilkinson has suggested various ways in which their curricula and forms of organisations were functionally well suited to transmitting the public service, gentleman ideology. Like the colleges established to train aspirants for the Church and the Army, the schools took a wide view of their educational responsibilities, aiming to socialise pupils into an ideal and total social role. Initially they seem to have concentrated on that aspect of their function at the expense of actual teaching. At any rate the Civil Service Commissioners were for some time distressed at the poor quality of many of their candidates.[57] Probably this also reflected the novelty of the system and perhaps the initial low demand for civil service posts. More reliable evidence for the educational failings of the early public schools was the development of many private 'crammers'. These aimed to teach what was necessary to pass the competitive examinations and secure entry to the service desired. The evils of 'cramming' caused considerable concern to those administering the competitive system. They had hoped to test ability, not rote learning. Again, however, it was partly a transitional problem. The 'crammers' flourished in the period before the system achieved equilibrium when the schools and universities had geared themselves to examination needs.

The older universities were also brought into this career system. The universities were communal institutions, emphasising extra- as well as intra-curricular activities but lacking the hierarchical discipline and organisation of the public schools. Before the reforms in the middle of the century, they had provided a venue in which the sons of the social élite could participate in a common style of life in which knowledge and learning played little part. Halsey's description of the universities in the eighteenth century as 'status differentiating agencies for an aristocratic structure of domination' is misleading only in so far as it suggests they played an active and important role as agencies of social selection and socialisation. This is what they appear to have acquired in the second half of the nineteenth century, as symbolised by such changes as the introduction of the examination system. These developments were a response to changes in the social structure which threatened the stable pattern of status groups and different life-styles in which they had been located. The examination system was a mechanism which could be used actively to select members for the social élite.

According to Rothblatt, the universities developed an ideology of public service and gentlemanly professionalism, similar to that

50

found in the public schools, to justify their role as agencies of social selection and socialisation.[58] The universities were to be centres of liberal education, fitting their students for leadership in government and administration, equipping them with the ideal of public service and enabling them to take their place in cultured society. Throughout the second half of the nineteenth century the universities gradually became more concerned that their students should find appropriate places in society. They began to prepare students for the competitive examinations and to show concern about employment opportunities for graduates in the Church and the professions. By the end of the century an employment agency had been established at Cambridge and dons were even beginning to consider the possibility of students entering on a business career. Rothblatt points out that by then some commentators had begun to comment on the difference between the new-style salaried executives in business and the older family businessmen who had presided over the early stages of industrial development. Some concluded that the liberal education designed for leaders in other fields might also be useful or desirable for the new type of business leader. Jones and Jenkins' study of Cambridge alumni in the eighteenth and nineteenth centuries shows that while the proportions attracted into the Church or able to go into such non-occupational fields as land-owning declined dramatically during the nineteenth century, there were small but consistent increases in the proportion going into the professions, administration, banking and business.[59] Rothblatt quotes a passage from J. S. Mill's Inaugural Address, given in 1867 at the University of St Andrews, in which he expounds clearly the new rationale for the universities, and contrasts the development of the 'whole man' with the occupational specialisation which might follow.

The proper function of an University in national education is tolerably well understood. At least there is tolerably general agreement about what an University is not. It is not a place of professional education. Universities are not intended to teach the knowledge required to fit men for some special mode of gaining their livelihood. Their object is not to make skilful lawyers, or physicians, or engineers, but capable and cultivated human beings. . . . Men are men before they are lawyers, or physicians, or merchants, or manufacturers; and if you make

51

them capable and sensible men, they will make themselves capable and sensible lawyers and physicians.[60]

But while the university leaders justified the role of the universities in developing much the same general qualities as were prized by those organising the competitive examination systems, university teachers were beginning to take seriously their own responsibilities for teaching, examining and research. The corollary of the universities acquiring a social function was the development of professionalism among those who could claim to be skilled in the performance of that function. The underlying contrast between the liberal ideal and the specialisation and professionalisation of university teaching and academic knowledge provides a graphic illustration of the twin strands in professional development, status professionalism and occupational professionalism. Rothblatt's account of late nineteenth-century Cambridge highlights the interdependence of the two processes. Initially the university teachers appear to have been locally oriented, making their career within their college and university and concentrating on their role in teaching and operating the mechanisms of socialisation and social selection. Some of the problems inherent in the two contrasting developments only became apparent with the appearance of the academic-subject specialist, oriented towards a career in his subject and expecting to move from institution to institution. This further development of occupational professionalism among university teachers has made it difficult for them to meet the demands of the liberal ideal. The difficulty of reconciling the two is still a key problem in the organisation of modern universities.[61]

The Professions in Industrial Society

The ideology of liberal education, public service and gentlemanly professionalism was elaborated in opposition to the growth of industrialism and commercialism. This is one reason why it drew so heavily on the older tradition of gentlemanly leisure and the established professions. It incorporated such values as personal service, a dislike of competition, advertising and profit, a belief in the principle of payment in order to work rather than working for pay and in the superiority of the motive of service. These

52

values closely resemble many of the characteristics which later commentators and sociologists have taken to be the defining characteristics of professions. Because of this, Rothblatt's thesis that in the context of the universities at least such values grew out of an alliance between the landed classes and the professional classes assumes particular importance. The status professions had long held themselves to be appendages of the gentry and had taken over many features of the gentleman ideal. The education system of the late nineteenth century recruited members of these classes into a governing élite, unified and supported them with a common ideology, and discouraged them, together with any recruits from business backgrounds, from embarking on commercial or industrial careers.

Earlier in this chapter we stressed that neither occupation nor education had great importance in determining status in pre-industrial society. Education became important as a mechanism of social selection at the same time as occupation became necessary as a claim to a position in the new middle class. The mechanism of educational selection seems to have been particularly necessary in a situation of social transition. It had only marginal importance in the previous situation of social stability. The same argument can be used to account for the wide view of their responsibilities for socialising pupils and students taken by the educational institutions in the new system. The ideology of professionalism was elaborated in opposition to the economic theories of industrial capitalism, but it was a mediating ideology. It called on business to recognise its limitations but not for the overthrow of the industrial system itself. It contributed to a process of gradual adaption rather than radical change. In the hands of the guild socialists or R. H. Tawney it could be allied to socialist or social democratic theories and turned into a more comprehensive critique of the economic and social system. But for most of those who went into politics or government service, the ideology simply called on them to keep their distance from business. It united them into a governing élite, sharing common beliefs and a common life-style.

Although it is frequently suggested that the nineteenth-century pressure for utilitarian reform and for open entry to public positions through competition came from representatives of the new middle classes, it is important not to exaggerate the part which businessmen and their families played in the process at this stage.

Businessmen were not immediately incorporated into the governing élite, nor were they immediately attracted to send their children to public schools or to one of the older universities. Undoubtedly some sought social position for their offspring through a university career, but Jones and Jenkins found that only 12% of Cambridge alumni in the second half of the nineteenth century came from business backgrounds, with another 3% who had fathers in banking and insurance.[62] By 1937–1938 the total figure for these two groups had shot up to 46%. Throughout the century the largest proportion of students came from clerical homes and this proportion remained roughly constant. A drop in the proportion coming from the gentry and land-owning classes was matched by small increases in the proportion from professional homes.

Guttsman's study of the British political élite presents a similar picture of initial middle-class advances being made by professional men rather than by businessmen or industrialists.[63] Throughout the second half of the nineteenth century the number of members of the House of Commons and the number of Cabinet ministers from aristocratic families declined sharply. But although there were a few Cabinet ministers from business backgrounds throughout the period, the majority of the middle-class ministers who filled the aristocrats' places were lawyers and professional men. Looking at a sample of these ministers in detail, Guttsman found that most had been to university, more than half to either Oxford or Cambridge, and just under a quarter had been to public schools. But Guttsman also points out that there were many businessmen in the House of Commons by the end of the century in spite of their exclusion from ministerial office. To suggest they were excluded from office in relation to their numbers draws attention once again to the contrast between the professional, service ethic of the governing élite which opposed the norms of business and commercialism.

The public schools too were initially institutions for consolidating the values of the landed and professional classes rather than for assimilating or socialising the sons of businessmen and manufacturers. Rothblatt makes the point that the success of Arnold's Rugby was not founded on the children of the new manufacturing classes. He quotes a study of public school recruitment in the first half of the century by Bamford which shows that pupils were mostly drawn from the aristocracy, the gentry, the clergy and the professions.[64] Initially, then, it seems that the system of educational socialisation and recruitment developed as an attempt to maintain the position of groups already enjoying high status and power in the society. It was a response to change in the sense that the structure of wealth and of the class and status systems in society were undergoing a radical change. But it was a response designed not so much to assimilate the consequences of these changes as to hold them at arm's length. Eventually the two branches of the middle class had to come to terms with each other and the educational system of social recruitment then played an important part in the process. As mentioned above, nearly half the graduates of Cambridge were drawn from business homes by 1937–1938 and nearly a third were setting out on business careers. At the same time the older universities still dominated recruitment to the higher Civil Service and the public schools dominated recruitment to the universities.[65] But even by the end of the nineteenth century as many as one-fifth of the entrants for the civil service competitions were from business families. The proportion of entrants for the military competitions was only slightly lower. Assimilation took place, but only gradually, and the ideology of service and professionalism played an integral, if transitional, part in the process.

An interesting sidelight on the strength of this ideology and particularly on its emphasis on culture, leisure and gentility is the fact that the Victorian middle-class public was able to support a group of professional 'men of letters', critics and columnists who were able to support themselves almost completely from their literary work.[66] The number of people giving their occupation as 'author' in the census enumerations rose from less than 200 in the census of 1841 to nearly 14,000 by the end of the century.

Artistic creators and performers were one group of professional occupations which showed a marked increase throughout the century. So too did the group of occupations concerned with land and land management – the architects and surveyors, for example, and the group providing technical and commercial services to business and industry, such as engineers and accountants. These two groups, which not only grew in numbers but organised themselves in study and qualifying associations, provide the important examples of the growth of occupational professionalism, based on specialised work.[67] Recruitment to the established professions remained relatively static throughout the century, though a group

55

of ancillary medical occupations began to aspire to be recognised as professions.

But it is easy to overlook the numbers and importance of the clergy throughout the period. At the beginning of the century they were numbered in four figures, while the physicians and barristers were small groups of no more than a few hundred each. The clergy maintained their numbers relative to the increase in the general population throughout the century. It was not until the early 1900s that a relative and then absolute decline in clerical recruitment set in. But their overwhelming domination of the educated and professional classes had been threatened much earlier. In later chapters we shall have occasion to return to the peculiar history of the clerical profession. Developments in this century show the occupation and the institutions of the Church continuing to adapt to the decline of status professionalism and to the search for occupational specialisation.

In this chapter we have suggested that professionalism at the end of the nineteenth century was a composite product of two trends. On the one hand there was a professional tradition claiming a right to social position rather than responsibility to perform any particular function. This claim was supported by a cultured and gentlemanly ideology and style of life. On the other hand changes in knowledge, economic and social organisation created opportunities for occupations to meet specialised demands. Such professions seem to have been anxious to assert their knowledge and competence as a support for their claim to economic security and professional standing.[68] Two rather different examination systems emerged, one testing professional knowledge and competence and the other providing a formalised and more 'open' method of testing for the symbols associated with a traditional claim to high social status. The medical profession provides a particularly interesting example of the interaction of these two processes in the gradual movement towards unity between the different branches of the profession. Traditional status professionalism played an important, if not dominant, part in setting out a professional ideology at the end of the nineteenth century. Professionalism in contemporary society is based on occupational specialisation, but new professions have drawn on the ideology and models of organisation set out in the older tradition, just as the older professions have developed directly from it. The prob-

56

lems of reconciling these two types of professionalism are still apparent in contemporary society and in later chapters we shall return to the question of the relevance and significance of the traditional ideology to new situations.

3 Selection, Recruitment, Education and Training

Professional Income and Prestige

Some professions are among the most prestigious and highly rewarded occupations in modern society. Studies of occupational prestige in Britain and the United States have consistently shown that the older professions are still accorded the highest status.[1] Professional income is also higher than average. Blau and Duncan found in their study of the occupational structure of the United States that the self-employed professionals were the occupational group with the highest average annual income.[2] There was a striking difference between their income, $12,048 p.a. in 1962, and that of business managers, $7,238. Blau and Duncan point out that the category 'managers' includes a small business élite which is probably more affluent and more powerful than the professional group, but it was too small to appear separately in their survey. The group of affluent professionals is larger, more widely dispersed through the community and so more visible as a privileged group to others in society.

In Britain and America there is a sharp difference between the incomes of those in the older, self-employed, or 'higher' professions, and those in the newer or 'lower' professions. The latter are generally salaried employees.[3] In the United States the salaried professionals had an average income slightly lower than that of the managers in 1962, $6,842. In Britain in 1960 'lower' professionals earned an average of £847 p.a. compared with £2,034 p.a. for 'higher' professionals and £1,850 for managers and administrators. These figures are not directly comparable to those of Blau and Duncan. Routh's study of earnings distribution omits the employers and proprietors, some of whom may be assumed to belong to the British business élite. In the United States there appears to be a large differential between the average self-employed professional and business income, in Britain the differen-

58

tial between higher professional income and managerial income is narrow and, in relative terms, declining. This may reflect the economic importance of self-employed status.[4] But these figures, giving the average income for broad occupational categories, obscure wide variations within each general group. For example, the 'higher' professionals in Britain includes the clergy with an average income in 1957 of £582 p.a. and barristers, solicitors, doctors and dentists who all had an average income of five times that amount in 1960.

In this century and the last the 'higher' professions have tended to do little more than maintain their size. Growth has been confined to the 'lower' professions and professionals. Although it seems clear that there has been some increase in the number of professionals, the exact rate depends on the precise definition given to the term 'profession'. Continual redefinitions of the occupational categories used in census enumeration do not help attempts to trace long-term trends.

One indicator which to a large extent side-steps these problems of definition is that provided by Millerson in his study of professional associations.[5] In Britain the formation of professional qualifying associations began in the middle of the nineteenth century. They continued to be founded at the rate of about twelve new associations per decade between 1880 and 1910. During the next forty years the rate of increase doubled. In the nineteenth century the new associations were mainly for engineers, accountants or those performing some service connected with the development or transfer of land. In the twentieth century, while new associations were still formed in these areas, managers and administrators and medical auxiliaries also began to found such associations.

But the growth in the number of associations cannot be taken as direct measure of the number of professionals. It also reflects internal differentiation within particular occupation groups. For example, Millerson found in 1950 that the largest number of associations were to be found in engineering, followed by management/administration and accountancy. But the census enumeration for the following year shows that teaching was the largest professional occupation, employing over 300,000 people and making up just over one-quarter of all professionals. Engineers accounted for just over one-fifth, with nearly 250,000 people. If only male professionals are counted, however, the relative size of these two groups is reversed.

Engineers and scientists are two professional groups which have substantially increased both in absolute numbers and relative to the increase in the size of the professional group as a whole. The older professions, however, have tended to decline relatively if not absolutely. The sharpest relative decline has been in the religious group. Overall the number of religious ministers has remained roughly stable since the turn of the century. But this overall stability conceals a relative decrease from just over a tenth to under a twentieth of all professionals, and obscures an absolute decline in the recruitment of ministers in many Churches.

The number of professionals has increased rapidly throughout this century relative to the general increase in the size of the labour force, but as a percentage of the total labour force the number of professionals is still small – just over 6% in 1951. Routh, in his study of occupation and pay in Great Britain between 1906 and 1960, found that the greatest increase over that period was in the number of clerical workers, followed by professionals and those in supervisory positions.[6] Employers and managers and all types of industrial worker showed considerably lower rates of growth.

The new professionals also differ from the old in another important respect – that of employment status. The proportion of professionals who were working on their own account, either as employers or as self-employed individuals, has declined sharply relative to the growth in the number of professional employees. Routh records that in Britain only the legal profession, among the older professions with a tradition of private practice, still had a majority of independent professionals in the 1950s. Overall the proportion of higher professionals working on their own account declined from 34% in 1931 to 18% in 1951, or as Routh notes, 13% if the doctors are counted as employees rather than self-employed within the National Health Service.

It seems generally true that professions make up a larger proportion of the labour force in more developed countries, but Ben-David has questioned whether there is any direct relationship between that proportion and the rate of economic growth.[7] He suggests that in countries where the proportion of professionals is large relative to other countries at a similar stage of development, such as the U.S.S.R., or small, such as India, the variation is to be explained by the social policies which have been adopted, rather than by any necessary relationship between professionalism and economic development. Direct comparison of the proportion of professionals in different countries is made even more difficult by problems of definition than comparison within a single country over time.[8]

These general figures on income level and occupational size suggest that the members of some professions are a highly privileged group in modern society. But the question whether professionals, or a particular group of professions, constitute an economic and social élite can be answered with greater precision by considering whether other common experiences and institutions tend to shape them into an élite group. One focus of this chapter is the process of recruitment into professional occupations. By examining the extent to which these occupations have been and still are self-recruited, or recruited from a particular class or status group within society, it will be possible to show whether there is a professional élite, supported by a differential process of recruitment and selection. Later in this chapter we shall take up the question of whether this process has important consequences in socialising professionals into social or occupational roles. Subsequently it will be important to consider whether there are any signs of professional class consciousness and what access professionals possess to centres of economic and political power.

One of the recurrent themes in the sociology of the professions has been the problem of where to fit the professionals in the general class and status structure.[9] Study of professional recruitment, socialisation, practice and organisation can show how far the professionals constitute a distinct, closed élite group sharing common beliefs about their situation on the basis of common experience. But as Marx said of the peasants, a group may share common experiences and still not be a class in the full sense of a group united in belief and action in society.[10] Professionals may share common experiences but these may well have divisive consequences for any general professional class or social élite. The emphasis on separation, autonomy and the individual career as distinct features of the professional type might suggest that professionals can form nothing more than a status group, in the Weberian sense of a group whose members happen to occupy a similar position in the social hierarchy.[11]

61

One of the strongest traditions in post-war British sociology has been the study of selection and recruitment within the social structure. As well as looking at the problem of social mobility in general, sociologists have concentrated on the role of the education system as a mechanism of social selection and others have looked in detail at the origins and social composition of particular élite groups.[12] Although many of these studies need replicating to bring the data up to date – the Glass study on social mobility, for example, was conducted too early to include in the sample any affected by the 1944 Education Act – taken together they provide a fairly comprehensive picture of social selection. But while the general picture seems reasonably clear a great deal of detail is missing, particularly concerning the composition of individual occupations. This means that the attempt to put forward a model of four separate but overlapping systems of social selection is to some extent speculative and intended as a framework which may prove useful in future investigations.

Diagram 1

Systems of Social Selection

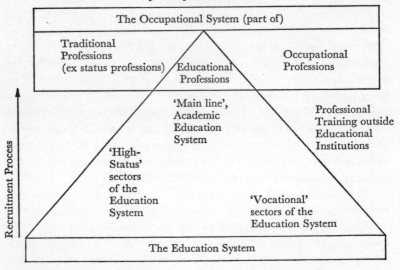

These overlapping systems are set out in Diagram 1. The model as summarised in this diagram is a considerable oversimplification of a set of complex interrelationships within and between various social institutions. The most important oversimplification is that the diagram suggests too static and compartmentalised a picture. Tensions between different educational institutions, as well as within and between different professions as they respond to changes in knowledge, techniques or systems of organisation, are all important factors making for continuing change in the systems of social selection.

One of the aims of the model is to suggest that while the education system does play a central part in occupational recruitment, it is itself a heterogeneous system. While many members of all professions will have passed through the 'main line' academic education institutions, these do seem to have the important effect of encapsulating many of their recruits so that they take up careers within the education system itself. This is suggested by the central triangle in Diagram 1. Some educational institutions have strong historic links with the system of recruitment into some of the older and higher-status professions. This system developed at the end of the nineteenth century and was discussed in the previous chapter. In that chapter we also noted that many of the newer occupational professions developed their own systems of education and selection. There has been a tendency throughout this century for some of these professional systems to be incorporated into the general educational system. Technical occupations in particular have become involved in courses in colleges of technology. Such colleges have been given a variety of names and titles since the Second World War, but they still lack the prestige of the 'main line' institutions and those through which recruits were selected for the traditional professions. The different parts of the education system have been based on different ideas of the role and function of education itself. In the previous chapter we noted that educational institutions were brought into the system of selection for the status professions with the manifest function of testing and developing general ability. Education for the occupational professions, on the other hand, was explicitly vocational, developing from such specific, particularistic techniques as apprenticeship. In both cases a latent consequence seems to have been that status selection continued. In the first case this depended on restricted access to the

63

educational institutions, in the second on an older tradition of patronage, sponsorship and cost of qualification. In educational terms the first system assumed that training in a specific expertise could follow ratification of general ability and cultivation of the 'whole man'. The second was concerned more directly with providing the skills and techniques necessary for the professional work. There has been considerable resistance from many occupational professions to attempts to introduce more general educational aims. The 'main line' education system itself has tended to be uneasy about the compromises it has adopted between the two educational approaches. The philosophy of higher education is still dominant over further education, but continual institutional realignment shows the potential for conflict and change within the system. This is obscured by the static form of Diagram 1.[13]

But the general characteristics of the whole system limit the opportunity of any individual organisation to change or redefine its own role independently. Recognising that the model sketched in Diagram 1 would be different in the United States draws attention to one of the central general characteristics of British education. The British system, based on a tradition of early segregation between different types of schools, is divided vertically into a number of separate channels.[14] The American system, on the other hand, is predominantly unitary, but divided horizontally as students leave an educational institution and instead of moving on to another drop out into the job market. Again this is an oversimplification of a system which includes some side channels designed, as Clark has put it, with the express purpose of 'cooling people out'.[15] Moreover, the unitary character of American higher education is a relatively recent development, coinciding with the growing importance of educational qualifications in the job market.[16] It has replaced a system in which education was at the same time more heterogeneous and less important.

The model of social selection outlined above has emphasised the role of the education system as an intervening mechanism between status of origin and future occupational position. Although, as we have mentioned, there are still some occupations which bypass the institutions of the education system, these have developed their own mechanisms of control over occupational entry. In general the development of these intervening selection mechanisms might be expected to have reduced the rate of self-recruitment

64

and status recruitment in the professions.[17] Blau and Duncan, for example, conclude as a result of their study of trends in the American occupational structure that there is a fundamental tendency in industrial society to substitute universal for particularistic selection criteria.[18] They suggest that in America the importance of educational qualifications in social mobility has increased as the importance of status of origin has declined. But the situation in Britain is complicated by the association which persists between different sectors of the education system and different class and status groups. Studies of the selection and recruitment into one profession – the Church – appear to bear out the supposition that self-recruitment is declining and the social basis of recruitment widening. In medicine, on the other hand, a profession which has maintained both its prestige and its income level, and which is often taken as the current model of professional organisation, the rate of self-recruitment appears to have increased slightly during this century.

Recruitment to the Professions

Kelsall concluded from a study of self-recruitment in four professions, based on data from Cambridge and three Scottish universities, that a medical career has maintained or increased its attraction to medical sons. The proportion of such sons in the whole group of medical students appears to have increased. In a later survey Kelsall conducted, covering all British university entrants for the academic year 1955–56,[19] 17% of all medical students were the sons of doctors. For those at Oxford and Cambridge taken together, the proportion was 25%. A survey conducted for the Royal Commission on Medical Education 1965–68, showed by 1966 that just over one-fifth of medical students had medical fathers.[20] The proportion was highest among Oxford and Cambridge students and lowest in the provincial medical schools. There was a slight trend towards an increase in the rate of self-recruitment between the first-year students and those about to qualify. This trend was confirmed by comparing the results of the Commission's survey with a similar one conducted on final-year students in 1961. According to that survey the overall proportion of self-recruited students was 17.7% in 1961, similar to Kelsall's figure for 1955–56.

In contrast the Church has become less attractive to clerical sons. The rate of self-recruitment has fallen. This is one of the changes in the organisation of the Church which has prompted Coxon to suggest that the ministry is perhaps a rare case of an occupation which is de-professionalising rather than professionalising.[21] From the mid-eighteenth century to the beginning of the twentieth the proportion of clerical sons following their fathers at Cambridge declined by about 10% per half century from 80% in the period 1752–99 to 60% in 1850–99. Clerical sons made up 37% of the total of students entering the Church in this latter period. By 1937–38 the proportion had declined to 34% and two-thirds of the sons of clergy at the university were not training for the ministry.

These figures for Cambridge students become increasingly unrepresentative of the ministry as a whole, as other channels of entry had been developed. In 1962 Coxon's survey of all aspirants to the ministry who had been approved for training by the Central Advisory Council for Training for the Ministry, showed that less than a tenth (8.7%) had clerical fathers. But Coxon has shown that this overall figure masks important differences between two types of recruit into the ministry. These two types, termed by Coxon the 'normal' and the 'late', tend to enter the ministry at different stages in their careers and to use different entry channels. The 'normal' group are those who enter the ministry at the start of their occupational careers as soon as they have achieved the necessary qualifications. The 'late' group enter the ministry at a later stage. For them the ministry is not a first-choice consequence of their educational career but an occupation to which they are attracted later in life.

Comparing the two groups, Coxon shows that the 'normal' group are more likely than the 'late' group to possess the characteristics associated with the ministry as a status profession. Among these characteristics are length of educational experience, attendance at a public school, a university career at Oxford or Cambridge and having a clerical father. Nearly 13% of the 'normal' group had clerical fathers in 1962, compared with nearly 4% of the 'late' group. Coxon's discovery of these two different groups of clerical recruits has interesting implications for the study of

66

occupational choice in the professions, to which we shall return later in this chapter.

This review of recruitment in medicine and the Church has brought out the important part which a few high-status educational institutions, notably the public schools and the older universities, have played in maintaining the rate of self-recruitment. These same institutions have also helped to ensure that professionals generally are recruited from the high-status groups in society. In 1955–56, between 28 and 30% of all students came from manual workers' families. The proportion was very much lower in medicine (16–20%).[22] Only the proportion in dentistry (15–16%) was lower. At the other end of the scale the faculties of technology and pure science included larger than average proportions of manual workers' children.[23] Nevertheless, there was a strong demand to enter medicine. The proportion of non-admitted to admitted students was only larger in the biological and veterinary sciences. Comparing the social origins of the admitted to the non-admitted students, Kelsall found that medicine was one of the few subjects where the proportion of manual workers' sons decreased significantly between the non-admitted and admitted groups.

Kelsall was not able to explain this discrepancy from the survey data at his disposal, but the attitude of one at least of the professional bodies was revealed in the evidence given to the Royal Commission on Doctors' and Dentists' Remuneration, 1958. The Royal College of Surgeons pointed out :

. . . there has always been a nucleus in medical schools of students from cultured homes. . . . This nucleus has been responsible for the continued high social prestige of the profession as a whole and for the maintenance of medicine as a learned profession. Medicine would lose immeasurably if the proportion of such students in the future were to be reduced in favour of precocious children who qualify for subsidies from the local authorities and the state purely on examination results.[24]

The survey conducted for the Royal Commission on Medical Education 1968 shows that these fears have not been realised. The proportion of medical students whose fathers were in social class 1 and 2, as defined by the Registrar General, increased from

67

just under 70% of final-year students in 1961 to more than three-quarters (75.5%) of those in their first year in 1966.[25] This compares with the Robbins Committee's figure of 59% for all undergraduates in 1961. In 1966 just over half the medical students had been to a maintained secondary school, almost exactly the same proportion as Kelsall had found ten years earlier. These continuing trends in the composition of the medical student population occurred during a period in which the numbers of pre-clinical students admitted rose only slowly and the numbers of newly qualified doctors remained almost stable. In 1957 the Willink Committee had diagnosed a possible surplus of doctors and advised a cut in the medical school intake.[26] Less than ten years later the Todd Commission reached the 'inescapable conclusion', as a result of their review of medical manpower in 1965–66, that Britain had faced a serious shortage of doctors and would continue to do so.

Figures as comprehensive as these for the medical profession are hard to come by for other professions. The medical data itself is only a beginning for a complete sociological study of the mechanisms within and outside the profession through which its size and composition are maintained. Kessel, in a study of the American Medical Association, has argued that its structure and practices are designed to secure artificial monopoly conditions for the medical profession.[27] One mechanism through which this cartel-like position is maintained is through control over entry. The strange contradiction between the findings of the Willink and Todd committees suggest that this topic would repay investigation in Britain. What is clear, however, is that although medicine is no longer the leisured status profession of the eighteenth-century physician, new entrants are drawn predominantly from the higher-class and status groups in society. A few high-status educational institutions play an important though by no means overwhelming part in this process. Nevertheless, the fact that half the medical students pass through the State secondary school system shows how much overlap there is between the selection systems set out in Diagram 1.

Within the education system it can be shown that the proportion of students from middle- and upper-class homes rises directly with the status of the educational institution itself.[28] It is less clear whether this linear pattern can be applied to courses organised by professions themselves, outside the institutions of the education

68

system. One interesting piece of information can be culled from the Robbins Report. In a detailed study of the four largest qualifying associations, the Committee found that most members of these associations had finished full-time education before they were eighteen. But in each case a large proportion had not been educated in State secondary schools.[29] Although these professions make their own arrangements for education and selection outside the educational system, it is by no means certain that this widens the social base from which they recruit their members.

The research quoted above on the origins of students studying science and technology suggests that professions based on science and technology would be among the most likely to have a wider social composition. Gerstl and Hulton, in a study of one part of the heterogeneous engineering profession (the Mechanical Engineers), found there was considerable diversity among the members of that part itself in routes of entry, type of work and work situation.[30] Nearly a quarter of the graduate members of the Mechanical Engineers' Society and nearly a half of the non-graduate members had fathers in manual occupations. At the other end of the scale 40% of the graduates came from professional or executive homes – a proportion considerably lower than that quoted above for undergraduates as a whole. The proportion of non-graduate members with professional or executive fathers was even lower – 20%, and the overall proportion with fathers in engineering only 4%. Comparing the older members of the sample with the younger, Gerstl and Hulton suggest there has been a tendency for the social composition of this profession to widen during this century.

University teaching is another profession in which the basis of recruitment has been widening, though this tendency seems to be of more recent origin.[31] In all but the arts faculties in the universities a decreasing proportion of the teaching staff has come from upper middle-class homes, or been educated in public schools and at Oxford or Cambridge. The reasons Perkins gives to explain his findings draw attention to the encapsulating effect of the education system itself. This was highlighted as a separate selection system in Diagram 1.

University teaching is especially attractive to first generation and other secondary school pupils and to first generation university students, the children of less educated but socially ambitious fathers, probably because it is, by the time they graduate, a familiar, secure profession which satisfies ambitions which have until then taken mainly academic shape and which requires no capital, family connections or parental income to bridge several years of lowly paid pupillage.[32]

Teaching as a relatively uninstitutionalised profession has long been credited with a crucial intermediary position in social mobility, especially in the longer perspective of mobility over two or three generations. It seems likely, as Perkins suggests, that the first generation to achieve educational success in a family will be particularly liable to encapsulation within the education system itself. Such children lack the family connections or support to provide alternatives to the goals and values suggested by the educational institutions. Jackson and Marsden made the same point as a result of their study of working-class grammar school children in Huddersfield.[33] Out of a total sample of 88, 46 ended up teaching, mainly in primary and grammar schools. 'Even amongst those who did take up other jobs there were a number who felt they had made a mistake in leaving the academic life, and looked back with longing to teaching as a "safe" career.'[34]

Marsden and Jackson provide a graphic account of the way in which these children were separated from their home environment and absorbed into the education system itself.

To begin with there was the grammar school to be chosen . . . knowledge as to the best and second best only circulated freely in those families with some history of grammar school education or with middle class connections. Many of the other parents had obviously been quite concerned, but both ignorant and embarrassed at their own ignorance.[35]

The child was out on its own, moving into worlds to which the parents had no access.[36]

. . . when so many other things seemed unsure work was basic, clear, markable. Success here was a peculiarly potent security, and even those children who refused to identify themselves with the school, largely identified themselves with the work.[37]

70

Most of the children were late in deciding on a career but 75 out of the original 88 went on to university or training college. . . . of those who went to college or university a large number were thinking of teaching . . . it was the 'drifters' who began to make up the bulk of the future teachers . . . they turned to teaching not because, deep at heart, they wanted to do it – but because they did not want to move away from the academic succession (eleven plus – 'O' level – 'A' level – college – teacher) which had become so entwined with their very sense of who they were in society.[38]

The picture of professional selection and recruitment which emerges is that of a variety of channels heavily skewed towards the high-class and status groups in society. The main exceptions which allow some access to members of local social classes seem to be the technological professions and those associated with the education system itself. It should be apparent that much of the evidence used to reach this assertion is suggestive rather than conclusive. More work is required before we have a clear picture of the structure of social selection, let alone of the mechanisms of selection themselves.

Occupational Choice/Occupational Commitment

So far in this chapter we have looked at social selection from the point of view of the professions. Jackson and Marsden's account of the way their working-class children were drawn into teaching at various levels directs attention to the other side of this process – the process whereby individuals are attracted to choose one occupation rather than another. From the point of view of the individual the process of recruitment has often been conceptualised as occupational choice. Study of this phenomenon raises much wider questions in sociology about the place of individual acts and choices within social structure and process. In spite of the common currency of the phrase 'occupational choice', such events are singularly difficult to isolate for any individual. At any given point an individual is not starting with a blank sheet in a perfect job

71

market, comparable to the perfect market of classical economic theory. Rather he is developing and extending on decisions and actions taken in the past which have brought him to his present situation.

One model of occupational choice has suggested that the range of alternatives available to an individual are progressively limited until eventually choice takes place within a relatively narrow range.[39] Ginzberg and his associates, developing a similar model, have emphasised that it is very difficult to reverse or change direction within this process of limitation.[40] At a later stage an 'achieved' characteristic like educational attainment becomes fixed, in the same way as an 'ascribed' characteristic such as status or origin. But the concept of choice can be questioned even harder by recognising the limited information available to most intending entrants to an occupation and the continuing importance of the social milieu in which their identity is established.

In a university setting, for example, ideas about future occupations will circulate among students. The occupational intentions of the students themselves may play a part in structuring these ideas. Occupational intention is likely to be an important part of the student's social identity within the student culture. Beardslee and O'Dowd used a semantic differential scale to investigate the profiles of the members of various professions and of students intending to enter these professions.[41] They found very large correlations between the 'stereotypes' of the practitioners and of the intenders. In another study Beardslee and O'Dowd showed that it was the student culture rather than the 'formal' culture of the faculty which was the important source of these images. They conclude : 'One striking effect of a climate of opinion is to influence perception by others of a person who carries the symbols that are the key to the opinion system. . . . This process works in two directions : not only may the individual apply a stereotype to others, but also he may mould his own behaviour to conform with common experience.'[42]

Becker and Carper in a study of occupational recruitment among three different groups of postgraduate students – intending engineers, physiologists and philosophers –show how different occupational identities develop within these groups.[43] The engineering students had thought of themselves as intending engineers for some time. Many left before completing the course to take up an attractive job offer. The internal culture and the outside world, in the form of parents and potential employers, supported their occupational identity. By contrast the physiology students had had to reorient themselves towards a new occupational identity. Most of them had been prevented from going through with their original intention of a medical career. Physiology did not become a visible alternative until they were well into undergraduate studies. Supported by the faculty who often attracted them into the field and then sponsored them for future employment in the limited range of openings available, they developed a strong identification with physiology, seeing it as providing the basis on which doctors would practise medicine. The philosophy students were different again. In their case there was a lack of occupational commitment and identity. The philosophy students were academically oriented and tended to have taken up philosophy to avoid an occupational commitment. As the course progressed they came to realise that they were committed by default to an academic career though they remained vague about the tasks and role attributes which would be expected of them as academics or philosophers.

Becker and Carper's account of the different ways in which these students developed occupational identities and became committed to a particular occupational career highlights the impact of different aspects of their social situations. But rather than describing mechanistically the influence of factors upon the individual, the way the range of possibilities open to him is limited, Becker and Carper suggest an alternative view in which the individual acts within the situation as he perceives and interprets it. They stress the importance of relationships between faculty and students and between the students themselves in structuring these perceptions of the situation. They also emphasise the influence of the academic institutions in relation to other institutions in the job market and the various senses in which the student becomes specialised as he follows his academic career.

It is possible to interpret data on occupational choice itself in line with this account of the interaction between occupational identity and structural career. Rogoff, for example, found that most medical students reported their decision to enter medicine as occurring at a time when they had made some public step towards specialisation in preparation for a medical career, for example enrolling in pre-medical courses.[44] But, adding a dynamic

73

perspective, Kandell found that students tended to up-date the time of their decision to enter medicine.[45] As they passed through medical schools, students continually revised their ideas of what it was they had decided to be as well as passing new milestones along the route to setting up practice as a doctor. Thus although Rogoff argues that the decision to enter medicine is a 'notably objective fact', in the sense that most students could report such a decision, it seems to be closely tied to crucial experiences in the pre-medical career.

An example of the way such crucial experiences may be conditioned by the culture of the occupational group itself to which the individual aspires is provided by Coxon's study of Anglican ordinands.[46] A 'call', the moment when the individual realises he has a 'true vocation' has a particular symbolic importance in entry to the ministry. It seems likely that retrospectively such symbolic experiences become important as the individual develops an occupational identity and begins to make sense to himself and others of his occupational career. When they occur, however, such moments seem more likely to be part of 'a series of situational decisions which individually have no rational connection with the choice of a particular occupation but, nonetheless, comprise the process of embarkation on a career.[47]

The concepts of commitment and career provide the link between this account of occupational recruitment and the discussion of social selection included earlier in this chapter. Three different processes of commitment – possibility commitment, cost commitment and social commitment – can be distinguished through which particular individuals from a limited range of social backgrounds are attracted into different professional occupations.

Possibility commitment occurs through the linking of social institutions in recognised career patterns so that the transition from one to another can be interpreted as specialisation towards a particular occupational career. Clements, in a study of occupational choice among children in all types of English selective State secondary schools, points out that the children

> did not choose from the whole range of occupations though they may not have realised this – their mental endowment and their social and educational milieu have established, within broad limits, the segment of possible occupations in terms of which

74

they think. It does not occur to the secondary modern boy that he might aspire to become a barrister, whilst the clever grammar school boy seldom entertains even the notion of becoming a semi-skilled mechanic and positive choices have been made from a restricted number of possibilities.[48]

As the individual specialises through following a particular institutional career, costs accumulate against a change of course. Becker, in his discussion of commitment as a general concept for explaining action, pointed out that people tend to make 'side bets' on the continuation of their present circumstances.[49] He cites as examples the occupational pension and the residential mortgage. But in a pre-occupational career cost commitment, in terms of the time and money invested in following a particular route, may be less important than the social commitment which results from the assimilation of occupational intentions into the individual's social identity. Both Rogoff and Coxon, for example, in their different fields found that early deciders reported support and encouragement from parents or adult friends already practising in the profession much more frequently than those reporting a later time of decision.

The concept of social commitment adds a dynamic perspective to role theory. Possibility commitment can also be seen in these terms. Even before an individual acquires a specific occupational intention he becomes committed to a role within a particular educational institution. This role will include a limited range of occupational intentions. It is of course possible for individuals to reject the identity made available to them through the educational institution.[50] This seems particularly likely where the individual is subject to conflicting pressures outside the institution. Similarly an identity and a social commitment may be formed in opposition rather than in accord with the known wishes of particular-role others. Conceptualising occupational recruitment as a process of commitment does not rule out the possibility of significant tension and conflict.[51]

The social composition of the professions therefore is a product, on the one hand, of these individual processes of commitment and, on the other, of the selection mechanisms used by the professions themselves. Possibility commitment or selection through the pre-occupational career has particular importance in the case of many

75

professions which require lengthy educational experience before an aspirant is admitted to practice. Subsequently in this chapter we shall consider some of the different characteristics of professional education in different institutional settings and some of the senses in which such institutions can be said to socialise recruits into a particular profession or a general professional élite.

Issues in Professional Education

In the whole field of the sociology of the professions, most attention has been devoted to the study of professional education and training. It is a convenient subject to tackle within the current institutional framework for sociological research. Professional educators are often more co-operative with researchers than members of other occupational groups. They can provide access to relatively captive populations from whom data can readily be obtained. Most sociological research is itself carried out in the setting of some institution of higher education, by individuals who have themselves experienced some form of professional training. Such practical considerations are one explanation for the preoccupation with studies of professional education and the relative neglect, as we shall see in the following chapter, of professional practice.

Nevertheless, studies of professional education raise important theoretical issues. Professionals as a whole, as well as the different professional occupations, can be seen as unique social groups, differentiated from the rest of society and characterised by distinct culture and patterns of behaviour. The autonomy allowed to the individual professional in his working life suggests that he needs to learn the practical techniques and the normative requirements of professional practice before he actually begins to work with clients. Normative socialisation of the professional is particularly necessary, so the argument runs, to protect the client from the misuse of professional authority.[52]

There is a danger of overestimating the amount of change which will be involved in the process of professional socialisation. Already in this chapter we have seen that professional recruits tend to be drawn from a limited range of backgrounds. Their status of origin tends to be very similar to the status to which they aspire.

76

But both these questions – how the individual is inducted into the culture of the professional group and socialised into the normative patterns of behaviour required for professional practice – also raise the wider issue of how in sociology it is possible to move from the study of present situations and behaviour to the prediction of the future behaviour of the same individuals in different situations. Much powerful sociological explanation tends to be situationally specific or at least confined within the framework of a static social system. Study of professional socialisation as a dynamic social process requires attempts to relate one situation to another, one system to another, over time.

The dimensions of this theoretical problem are well illustrated within the literature on professional education and socialisation. Some studies have concentrated on the impact of socialisation experiences on current behaviour in current roles. Others have attempted to link these experiences to future situations and future roles. Both the major projects on socialisation into the medical profession in the United States began by posing their problem in terms of the future role and role group to which the medical students aspired.[53] But while the Columbia studies continued to accept this focus throughout, at Kansas the focus switched to the role of student itself.

> The opportunities and disabilities of the student role are decisive in shaping the perspective students hold. . . . They do not act as young doctors might act, but rather act as students act. This overstates the case, for certainly medical students organise their actions with reference to a medical future. But what is important to remember is that this is a future, and, while in school, they are not doctors, do not face the problems doctors face, and consequently, cannot employ the perspectives and culture of doctors.[54]

The switch of attention towards the role of student is a switch to a present role and present activity carried on within the current organisational setting. The individual is being socialised into the role he already occupies. Socialisation involves learning to be what one already is, as well as learning to be what one will or might become. The dilemma has been captured by Goffman in the phrase 'doing is being'. In interpersonal interaction, or 'situated

77

activity systems', as Goffman calls them, the individual can readily slip into the role made available to him by the others in the system. 'Role', he writes, is 'the activity the incumbent would engage in were he to act solely in terms of the normative demands upon someone in his position.'[55] According to this model, behaviour is to be expected mainly by reference to short-run situational pressures. The individual is oriented to short-term goals. He has only to conform to situational pressures to adopt a ready-made self.

Goffman has applied this situationally specific mode of analysis to institutional structures and identified a general category of institutions, total institutions, in which common patterns of organisation and behaviour have developed, based on common situational features.[56] Total institutions are those in which the individual passes the whole twenty-four hours of his daily life-cycle. Examples range from concentration camps to ships at sea, from logging camps to public schools, from seminaries to mental hospitals. But, as Ward has pointed out, there is a crucial difference within this general category between organisations which have technical or instrumental goals like ships and logging camps, and those which endeavour to change the individuals within them. Goffman's general argument is that the total features of all these various institutions produce disculturation. The institution member is forced to abandon the culture to which he belonged before joining the institution. In so doing he becomes encapsulated within it. Patterns of behaviour develop based on the immediate situational pressures experienced within it. But the process is likely to be different in those institutions whose products are people rather than things and whose goals include bringing about some change in their members.

Various attempts have been made to establish predictive typologies of organisations in general and, more specifically, of educational and socialising institutions.[58] Such typologies have included a wider range of types and allowed for a wider range of outcomes than the single link made by Goffman between the characteristic of totality and the consequences of disculturation. The most important differences are those in organisational goals and in the way the organisation secures the compliance of its members. Bidwell and Vreeland, for example, make a distinction between role and status socialisation as organisational goals and

78

communal and associational involvement on the part of the client-members.

Role socialisation consists of training in the skills of a future role; status socialisation involves acquiring a more general social identity and patterns of behaviour acceptable to people in the future status position. There are limits as to how far these two types of socialisation can be separated. One usually involves the other. Nevertheless, the contrast between them is suggestive when combined with the distinction between different types of client involvement. Bidwell and Vreeland contrast two notional contracts which the client might make with an organisation. One contract, the utilitarian, is entered into for specific gains and rewards, for example educational qualifications. In the other, the normative, the individual accepts the broader goals of the institution and the cultural framework in which they are set. These two contracts have very different implications for the relationship between the leaders of an organisation and its client-members. A utilitarian contract implies that the client-member is himself in a position to judge whether the organisation is keeping its side of the bargain. A normative contract, on the other hand, tends to invest the organisation with absolute moral authority. Cross-tabulating these two dichotomies gives two polar types of education institution across one diagonal; the 'doctrinal community', similar to Goffman's total institutions, in which the goal of the organisation is status socialisation and the client-members' contract normative, and the 'procedural association', emphasising role socialisation and accepting utilitarian contracts.

In the field of professional education these two polar types may be illustrated by the military academy and the technical college. This raises the historical question of how these different types of organisation became associated with different professions. In the pre-industrial period recruits to the 'status professions' were exposed to status socialisation, often in communal organisations. It seems doubtful, however, whether such communal organisations as the old universities were 'doctrinal communities', with the strong, homogeneous moral impact, hypothesised by Bidwell and Vreeland. Socialisation was a latent rather than a planned function of such organisations, a consequence of association with fellows drawn from similar backgrounds in a wide range of activities far removed from formal education. As mentioned above, there is always a danger of assuming that socialisation means changing the individual rather than simply confirming and extending existing attitudes and patterns of behaviour. 'Occupational professions', on the other hand, placed much more emphasis on role socialisation, usually through some form of apprenticeship outside any institutional structure.

As 'leisured status' has become a less important characteristic of the professional and been replaced by specific expertise and competence, these two types of recruitment and education have tended to come together. Vocational content has been introduced into the general communal educational experience and attempts have been made to exercise more direct control over the outcome of such experiences in terms of both role and status socialisation. Conversely, more general educational courses within various types of educational institution have been widely introduced as a supplement to or a replacement for apprenticeship. The result is that most professional education now is not completely specific in content or setting nor is it completely void of vocational content, as were some routes into the 'leisured' professions in the eighteenth century. It takes place within organisations which include people other than practitioners, ex-practitioners or aspirants to a particular profession. It covers subjects which are not closely related to the skills and techniques of the future occupation as well as those which are.

There is still considerable variation between different occupations, however, and there are a few professions which have not followed one of these two paths. They have developed their own institutions for training and socialisation. In these, conditions approximate much more closely to those of the 'doctrinal community'. These 'differentiated' professions generally involve 'occupational situations in which the person's work is felt to be his whole life'.[59] Professional practice is carried out by people symbolically and often physically separated from the lay public. The military uniform and the clerical collar are examples of such symbolic separation in the two professions which provide clearest instances of 'differentiated' occupations in modern society. To adapt Goffman's terminology, these are the occupations in which the professional role is most total.[60] It is no accident that they should also be the occupations which have carried out education and training in the setting of total institutions.

80

Studying the military academy as a total institution sets in sharp relief some of the limitations of the situationally specific view of socialisation processes. Since the nineteenth century the officers in the military forces of both Britain and the United States have been trained in specialised military academies. Masland and Radway, in their examination of American military education, have pointed out that the academies ensure institutional and cultural continuity in the armed services.[61] As Janowitz has remarked, however, indoctrination in the Army depends not simply on academies and formal entry procedures, but also on 'the daily routine of military existence'.[62] But the Services themselves seem to believe that the academies provide important formative experiences and lay the foundations for their particular officer corps. In the United States the Navy rejected the suggestion that all three Services should share a common academy for officer training, not for educational reasons, but because they thought the Naval Academy at Annapolis had a unique role to play in creating élite officers for the élite service.

The study of the Academy of the United States Coast Guard Service, carried out by Dornsbuch, predates Goffman's general account of the total institution.[63] But it raises many of the same issues, in particular whether such an organisation can go beyond 'institutional socialisation' to bring about 'life-cycle socialisation' – that is have an impact on the individual's behaviour in future as well as present roles.[64] In Goffman's terms, the 'presenting-self' of the new recruits was effectively destroyed during the first year at the Academy. The 'swabs' or new recruits were separated from the outside world, immersed in the routine of the institution and subject to continuous degradations.[65] These mortified the self and separated the 'swab' from his previous social role and identities.

But it appears from Dornsbuch's account that as the 'swabs' lost their old social identities, they began to acquire a new one as cadets and future members of the Coast Guard Service. They tended to see their career in the Academy as a short and necessary period leading to a desired and definite goal, entry to the Service.[66] Recruits in different years were not rigidly isolated from their seniors by differences of role and seniority. As well as regular

81

opportunities for contact there was a day once a year when the 'swabs' were allowed to change roles with those in the middle years – a practice which, as Goffman has noted, is particularly common in 'total institutions'. The cadets came to value their separation from the outside world and to develop a sense of pride and self-esteem in their differentiated role as cadet and future officer in the Coast Guard Service. Myths and rumours circulated within the student body about in-service hostility and competition between academy-trained officers and those commissioned from the reserves. This sharpened the cadets' awareness of themselves as a differentiated élite.

The result was that the Academy isolated the cadets from the outside world and then helped them to identify with their new role. In addition to 'institutional socialisation' the cadets were also subject to a process which Dornsbuch, following Park and Burgess, called 'assimiliation'. 'Assimiliation' is a 'process of interpenetration and fusion in which persons and groups acquire the memories, sentiments and attitudes of other persons and groups and, by sharing their experience and history, are incorporated with them in a common cultural life. . . .' The very experience of degradation as an aspirant to the group became later an important part of the group's own consciousness of its separate identity.

Dornsbuch's study does suggest that training in this type of institution has consequences beyond 'institutional socialisation'. Some of the most important aspects of the process seem to have been the serial progression involved in the institutional career, anticipatory socialisation towards a new social identity in the future occupational role and developing consciousness of the unique and differentiated features of that role. Relationships with other inmates – senior, junior and contemporaries – seem to have been a more important mechanism in this type of socialisation than the 'reciprocal role relation between teacher and student' which Bidwell and Vreeland identified as the 'central technology of education'.[67]

The Study of Professional Socialisation

Dornsbuch's approach to the study of socialisation focused attention on the individual in his social environment, not simply on the individual himself. A more individualistic approach has been widely used in studies of professional education and socialisation. This approach invokes a more atomistic view of man. Man tends to be regarded as a passive receptacle into which new characteristics can be placed. According to this view, during the socialisation experience the individual is equipped with various skills, norms, values and attitudes, necessary or relevant to future behaviour. The individual's equipment can be measured before and after the experience. This opens up a way of solving one of the most crucial difficulties in socialisation studies, that of linking present experience to future behaviour. This approach seems to have provided the main theoretical basis for the Columbia studies of socialisation in medical school. In contrast, the researchers at Kansas, though they seem to have been more ambivalent about the difficulty of socialisation being limited to present beliefs and behaviour within current situations, adopted a theoretical approach which stressed that such beliefs and behaviour – the culture of the medical students – arose from common current problems experienced by students within the structure of the medical school.

There were also methodological differences between the two studies. These differences suggest that even if methods are not a function of theory, or, vice versa, theory a function of methods, at least the two are closely interrelated. Both studies used a combination of participant observation and survey research, but while the former was the main method at Kansas, the latter was dominant in the Columbia research. In the Columbia studies the results of surveys and other structured methods based on a defined sample at a particular point in time form the basis of the report. Observers' notes and other less-structured material were used to supplement the picture. For the Kansas study, on the other hand, a team of researchers were attached to one class throughout their four-year course in graduate school. In the report the results of this extensive period of participant observation are only occasionally supplemented by the results of a small survey, conducted with a sample of all students at a particular point in time.

The Columbia researchers were not insensitive to the importance of general processes of social interaction in the socialisation experience. At one point Merton suggests that there may be a division of labour between didactic teaching leading to direct learning (role socialisation in Bidwell and Vreeland's terms) and

83

(status socialisation) indirect learning 'in which attitudes, values and behaviour patterns are acquired as by-products of contacts with instructors and peers, with patients, and with members of the health team'.[68] In a later report on further aspects of the Columbia studies, Merton and Christie use the concept of 'values climate', analogous to a meteorological climate within an organisation, to examine these processes of indirect learning.[69] But the methods they suggest for examining this climate involve measuring the values and attitudes of staff and students to assess the consistency of the values climate between those in different roles and those in different years.

Becker and his associates, on the other hand, argue that culture is not a distinct separable feature of the membership of a role group but that it arises directly from role performances and role relationships. In their theoretical formulation 'perspective' – defined as 'a co-ordinate set of ideas and actions a person uses in dealing with a problematic situation, a person's ordinary way of thinking and feeling about and acting in such a situation'[70] – serves as a linking concept between role and culture. Their view is that action in repetitive situations follows previously elaborated perspectives until a new problematic situation is experienced. This requires the formation of a new perspective. Situations are likely to be problematic in so far as they have not been met before and in so far as the choice they offer affect the ability of the individual or group to achieve their goals. Individual perspectives are elaborated into a shared culture when they can be used by a group of individuals in similar role situations as collective solutions to shared problems. Perspectives, while not situationally specific, are situationally located, unlike values and attitudes which may refer more or less closely to hypothetical situations but which are not seen as part of an ongoing process of situational response.

Individuals experience new situations as problematic according to their long-run perspectives, defining long-term goals. This idea of a long-run perspective is particularly important in the work of the Kansas researchers. It helps them to move beyond the situationally-specific view of socialisation.

Long-range perspectives are diffuse and generalised and do not state specific imperatives to be followed under specific conditions. Rather they suggest a mood in which one will approach

84

specific situations and generalised values one will try to maximise. But the immediate situations in which action must be taken constrain behaviour in specific ways and actors must come to terms with these immediate situational imperatives. . . . Long-range perspectives influence the actor's behaviour in so far as they are seen by the actors as relevant and possible to use.[71]

Methodologically there seem to be considerable problems in identifying such long-run perspectives and separating them from perspectives developed within any particular situation. Conceptually, however, they set the context for the development of short-run perspectives. They should re-emerge more distinctly at points where the individual changes from one role to another, from one situation to another.

An example of one way in which such long-run perspectives are modified through the experience of professional socialisation can be seen in the impact which new knowledge and contact with professional teachers and professional practitioners has on the initial stereotyped ideals which students have of their future professional role.[72] These stereotypes are usually derived from similar stereotypes available in the general lay culture. They stress the dramatic and public aspects of the professional role. For example, law students tend to think of the lawyer as a courtroom advocate doing battle for his client.[73] Medical students at Kansas had an 'outback' view of medicine. They expected they would be called upon to save life in a sudden, isolated emergency. Mauksh and Shuval confirm that in rather different societies nursing students think of the nurse as someone who helps, comforts and serves in emergency situations.[74] In each profession there are a variety of folk-models who epitomise these ideals. They are drawn from the heroes of the mass media (Perry Mason, Dr Kildare) or from professional history, selectively interpreted (Florence Nightingale).

Law students' ideas about the lawyer's role widen through their experiences at law school and even more from the 'reality shock' which follows as they enter professional practice. At Kansas, the doctors who taught the medical students in the hospital tried to combat the students' 'outback' image of medicine directly. They stressed that the modern doctor should beware of acting too independently. Efficient medical practice depended on scientific aids, hospital services and specialist knowledge. Most of the Kansas students were destined to go into general practice while their teachers were hospital specialists. Their different views of the medical role can be seen as directly related to different type of practice situation and the division of labour existing within the profession.

Entering students have some ideas in general terms about the nature of future professional practice. One function of the educational institution is to shift the emphasis between one set of ideas and another, adapting student goals contained in their initial perspectives, to the career opportunities available in professional practice. Structural features of the institution, and of the whole education system, can have this effect of channelling students towards some opportunities and away from others. This is the same phenomenon at a later stage which was discussed under the heading 'possibility commitment'.[75] An example is the stratification of American legal education which largely parallels the stratification of the American Bar.[76]

But there are also cases where the channels opened up by the educational institutions are out of step with the opportunities available in professional practice. At least one commentator on the British system of hospital-based medical education has argued that it is extremely disfunctional for a major section of the profession, who must go into general practice after graduation.[77]

> The present recruits to general practice were never trained, and seldom given any inkling of what goes on in the world outside the teaching hospital. When a person has a long and arduous training, and then is pitched out into another field of activity for which he has not been prepared, it is not to be wondered at that he suffers some measure of frustration and bewilderment.

In support of his argument, Hill quotes a survey of junior hospital doctors which showed that while between 40–50% would have to obtain employment in general practice, only $7\frac{1}{2}\%$ expressed any desire to do so.

This process of career development seems to be one in which the staff in the educational institution may play an important part. They are able to direct selected students towards specialised career opportunities. One of the consequences of increasing use of institutionalised socialisation settings, as noted by Wheeler,[78] has been the development in most professions of a separate group of professional educators. These are liable to develop a recruitment and career structure separate from that of the general professional practitioners. A current British example is the staffing of the colleges of education. There is a dilemma between recruiting newly qualified subject experts straight from the universities or ex-teachers who have professional experience but may lack the breadth of up-to-date knowledge. Further specialisation of career routes and opportunities is possible where a profession also engages in research. Teaching and research may become available to the students as alternative identities from that of professional practitioner. It is through this process of anticipation in acquiring new social identities that the structural features of institutions are converted into socialisation experiences.

Coxon's study of Anglican ordinands provides one example of the way different identities, current and anticipatory, may be available in training for the same profession.[79] Coxon's study was carried out in two theological colleges, one of which was closely attached to a university and the other of which was independent and had a larger proportion of older, married ordinands.[80] Coxon set out to test the hypothesis, which Huntington had verified for American medical students in the Columbia studies, that the longer the students had been in professional training the more likely they were to have a self-image of themselves as members of the profession.[81] In the case of the medical students, Huntington showed that this development was closely related to the type of role performance allowed within the student role and to the students' ideas of how others in their role set – notably faculty and patients – were behaving towards them. The ordinands, on the other hand, did not have any periods of practical training comparable to the clinical years of the medical student. Ordination after graduation from theological college marked a much more clearly defined moment of entry into professional practice. In contrast to the medical students, the ordinands were unable to think of themselves as professionals (priests) until after ordination. But Coxon found that the ordinands' self-image varied between 'student' and 'ordinand' according to the socialisation setting and the role of others with whom they were involved.

In the college attached to the university, ordinands thought of themselves as 'students' in relation to staff and students at the

87

university, and as 'ordinands' in relation to staff and other ordinands in the college and in relation to parents, friends and the parish priest at home. As Coxon points out, this ambiguous identity situation posed some problems of role-playing for the ordinands. The ambiguity was present but less marked in the other theological college not attached to a university.

The contrast between the ordinand and student self-images used by the Anglicant ordinands may be compared with the findings in the Kansas study that different medical students used two different perspectives, one based on a self-image as 'student' and the other on a self-image as 'medical student', to handle the problems of the two initial years of academic medical education. In the first two years the student's main problem was to deal with the vast academic work-load. Initially, students tried to learn everything which was put before them. This was based on their long-term perspective of themselves as future doctors. They believed all the knowledge would be valuable and necessary for future medical practice. But this solution became physically impracticable, so the students had to sort out a more limited range of material to learn. This they did, using one of two different perspectives. The 'medical students' continued to look towards future medical practice and to sort the material according to what they thought would be their most valuable. The 'students', on the other hand, tried to find out what the faculty thought they should know and in particular on what the faculty planned to test them. After the first-year examinations this became the dominant perspective. It was a more effective way of meeting the immediate demands set within the institution. Becker and his associates showed that initially students developed one or other of these perspectives according to their past experiences of the student role in university and according to their relationship with different groups in the medical school. Summarising broadly, the 'students' tended to have come straight from university, to have been members of fraternities there and to have been selected for fraternity membership in medical school. The 'medical students' were more often married, living off campus on a caravan site and so more individually isolated from the school and their fellows.

Becker and his associates did not expect the medical students to find a self-image as doctor useful or available within their situationally-defined, institutional roles.[82] A recent study of students in the science departments of British universities has suggested that the adoption of a particular occupational identity can offer a solution to other sorts of problems experienced by students within the educational institution.[83] In this study Box and Ford argue that working-class students in universities are liable to face an acute form of identity crisis. Science students can resolve this crisis by adopting the 'dedicated scientist identity' and orienting their work and career towards it. The acute identity crisis arises out of the contrast between the students' (working-class) culture of origin and the (middle-class) status and culture in which they are placed through university education. In this situation of social marginality the 'dedicated scientist identity' is available as a continuation of their career and experiences within the education system. It does not bring them into any new conflict with their culture of origin. It provides an example in microcosm of the way in which the general process of encapsulation within the education system, discussed above, can occur.

So far the material presented on professional socialisation follows or has been fitted into the interactionist approach, discussed above. The alternative, atomistic approach contrasts with this most clearly in the attempt to study normative socialisation. Merton, in his introduction to the Columbia studies, emphasises why normative socialisation is important :

. . . the physician in his private office is largely subject to the controls only of the values and norms he has acquired and made his own. The medically uninformed patient is not in a position to pass sound judgement upon the normative adequacy of what the physician does. Medically informed colleagues are not in a position to know what is being done. These structural facts, therefore, put a special premium on having these values and norms instilled in the student during the course of professional socialisation in the medical school. If this is not thoroughly achieved under optimum conditions provided by medical school, it is unlikely that it will occur under the less favourable circumstances of private practice.[84]

Through socialisation, students acquire built-in regulatory mechanisms. These can be measured as the norms, values and attitudes they hold. In collaboration with Christie, Merton has suggested various methods for researching into this problem.[85] Using a scale measuring 'Machiavellianism', Christie and Merton's preliminary findings were that medical students were on the average more 'Machiavellian' than 'a small sample of top-echelon business executives' and a sample of registered lobbyists in Washington. This bizarre discovery highlights some of the basic problems of the whole method. Members of different groups will translate the items of the scale into different practical situations. There is no means of controlling this link between abstract norm and social reality. The approach can only deal with the problem of relating present behaviour to future for the unique social situation of completing scale tests.[86]

Such work based on this atomistic approach to the socialisation process has the effect of reifying the individual's own attitude position without reference to present or future behavioural situations. On this view an analogy could be drawn between people-changing organisations and those producing material products. The product leaves the organisation equipped with the desired norms and values. They are carried forward to act as a separate source of behavioural regulation in future situations. The analogy breaks down because people are involved in a continual process of interaction with their environment. Attempts to measure values and attitudes seem to be based on a view of man springing from the traditional speculations of moral philosophy, not from the study of human behaviour in the social process. The idea that people refer immediate situational decisions to progressively more abstract and general standards and values is understandable in view of the long history of attempts to generate absolute moral standards in religion and philosophy. Sociologists might do better to pause and question whether people use such generalisations and analytic hierarchies in their social behaviour.

The techniques used in this type of research successfully give the impression that people do. They measure something, if only because they are designed to produce reified and quantified results. The problem of what is in fact being measured in such studies is highlighted by the negative results they often produce, when set to measure change over time. This applies not only to the study of the effects of socialisation experiences but also in such fields as the study of mass media effect.[87] The question remains whether such evidence should be accepted at face value. Perhaps it is a methodological consequence of trying to measure something which has little relation to the way people ordinarily live their lives. This discussion raises wider issues which can only be touched upon here. It shows, however, that an apparently parochial dispute over the study of professional socialisation hinges on issues of extremely general relevance and importance.

Merton has noted, as one of the problems facing anyone interested in studying socialisation into a profession, the fact that in the culture of the professional group

> . . . for each norm, there tends to be at least one co-ordinated norm, which is, if not inconsistent with the other, at least sufficiently different as to make it difficult for the student and the physician to live up to them both . . . medical education can be conceived as facing the task of enabling students to learn *how to blend* incompatible or potentially incompatible norms into a functionally consistent whole. Indeed the process of learning to be a physician can be conceived as largely the learning of blending seeming or actual incompatibles into stable patterns of professional behaviour.[88]

The norms which Merton goes on to include in a long list of incompatible pairs are taken from the public statements of professional bodies and practitioners. But to ask how students and physicians manage to live up to them both is to assume that that is what they are required to do; that such norms can be built into a cultural framework within which the individual must fit.

An alternative interpretation would be to take the evidence of normative inconsistency as it stands, as evidence of inconsistency. Such norms can then be seen as explanations or justifications of professional action readily available to a practitioner confronted with a variety of different role others in different situations. This interpretation follows the argument of Becker and his associates in the Kansas studies that group culture can be seen as a collective wisdom on how to respond to the problems of common experience.

The concept of socialisation has been used in a variety of ways in social science but usually with an emphasis on the way the individual can be shaped to fit into his social situation. Brim, for example, in a survey of 'socialisation through the life cycle', has summarised it as a process through which the individual shapes

91

and is shaped by society.[89] The normative approach to the study of socialisation discussed above seems to be based on the twin ideas that the individual develops internal regulatory mechanisms of social control and fits into the culture of his future role and status group. This approach can be criticised on a number of grounds – that it puts too much emphasis on shaping and fitting, that it implies a very passive view of man in society, that it appears to concentrate on the attraction of similar values and behaviour patterns at the expense of the clash of opposites, that it assumes a tendency toward harmony and equilibrium rather than an ability to live with tension and conflict in the dynamic of social process.

An alternative approach would be to retain the idea of sociali-sation but drop the automic coupling of the concept with the preposition 'into'. The question to ask, then, would be how does the individual learn to use elements in his social situation? The idea of 'using' just like the idea of 'shaping' also has wider implica-tions for the view which is taken of man as a social actor. 'Using' implies purpose. It directs attention towards the individual's goals, to his orientation towards the future, to his ability to act in relation to both the positive and negative influences in his environment. There is no need to assume that an individual must have such goals and orientations; simply that if he does they will play an important part in structuring the way he interprets his immediate situation and acts within it.

In the course of this chapter we have seen that such goals or orientations towards the future are especially important in bringing about change rather than institutionalisation through the sociali-sation experience. Their influence was perhaps clearest in the setting of the military academy, a total institution. The cadets were institutionalised, but that was only part of the story. It might be the whole story if the individual were unable to make use of his institutional experience. For example, in a penal institution an individual might lack goals himself or see little prospect of realising any change within the structure of the institution.[90] But in institu-tions of professional education immediate structural or situational problems cannot be isolated from students' beliefs about their future careers and their ideas about the demands which will be made upon them in their future situation. The argument that people act within situations, according to the requirements and relationships of those situations, is a powerful one which has been

92

demonstrated by research in many fields. Indeed, it can be erected into a slogan against attempts to moralise, proselytise or exhort people into adopting different behaviour – if you want to change people, change their situations. But people must interpret such situations. They must decide, in the terms of the Kansas study, what is a 'problem'. To know how they will do this, it is necessary to know who they think they are, where they have come from and where they think they are going.

Throughout this chapter we have emphasised the continuity between the various experiences to which the individual is exposed through the processes of recruitment, selection and socialisation. Socialisation itself can be treated as a form of selection through which the individual is directed, or learns to direct himself, along particular paths. The processes of commitment, identified above, continue through the period of institutionalised professional training. This training shapes and consolidates the aspirant's ideas on his future occupational identity. It makes some opportunities available to him, while denying him others. These processes continue after the period of formal training as the individual moves through various practice situations. One of the distinctive features of the professional type is the developmental process associated with the individual career. This will be examined in the next chapter in a discussion of professions in practice.

4 Professional Practice

The Idea of Professionalism

The professions have often been criticised for being over pretentious. Cynics have suggested that no matter how lofty the ideals, given a choice between ideals and self-interest, the latter would prevail. The fact that many of the ideals of professionalism can be shown to bear little relation to the circumstances of ordinary professional practice seems to support their argument. Earlier in this century, when some were prepared to put forward professionalism as a basis for a more just and rational society,[1] others countered that professionals were no better than other men and professional association little different from other forms of occupational organisation.[2]

In Chapter 2 we suggested that the twin spurs behind the elaboration of a professional ideal were the tradition of status professionalism and the historical circumstances in which occupational professionalism emerged as a contrast to industrial and commercial values. The ideal had three important aspects – the notion of service, an emphasis on professional judgement based on professional knowledge and a belief in professional freedom and autonomy in the work situation. These three aspects will also demand considerable attention in the course of this chapter. The aim of this chapter is not simply to explode this professional ideal as a myth. Unlike the social critic, the sociologist must recognise that the ideal itself is a real phenomenon. One of the sociologist's tasks is to explain the genesis and persistence of this ideal, and to trace its significance for established and aspiring professionals.

The prevalence of the professional ideal is one reason why the problem of definition discussed in Chapter 1 has loomed so large. One way round the problem is to look at professions in terms borrowed from role theory. An individual aspiring to professional status is surrounded by a cluster of expectations about the way he

94

should behave inside and outside the work situation. A variety of authors have identified a variety of characteristics as professional. If an individual adopts a professional frame of reference then these characteristics are the ones which will be available to him as guidelines by which to orient his activities. For example, he may recognise that as a professional he should remain emotionally detached, maintain his superiority over laymen, including the client, and not seek financial reward.[3] But he may not use this frame of reference all the time. Other guides to action may be available, based on other features of his personal and occupational situation. This is the perspective which will be developed in the course of this chapter. It is closely tied to the contrast in the previous chapter between situationally-specific and idealistic accounts of the socialisation process in the professions. It raises two questions, to be taken up below. In which occupations, under what circumstances, does the professional orientation become important? Secondly, at the level of the social structure rather than the individual or the occupation, what is it that makes professionalism continue to be viable in modern society?

One step towards an answer to this second question is to recognise that society has accepted in whole or in part some claims for separation and autonomy made by various occupational groups and by the individuals within them. It is this aspect of separation and autonomy for the profession and the professional, at various different levels within the social structure, which will be elaborated in the course of this chapter. This, it will be argued, provides the main basis for a distinct professional type. Different aspects of autonomy are included within the professional ideal, but they are also a consequence of the type of work, work relationships, associations and institutions in which the professional participates.

This is not to say that professional autonomy is to be taken at face value as an absolute factor in any situation. No claim is being made that professional behaviour and expertise should be treated as independent variables in the analysis of social relationships. On the contrary, the perspective outlined above specifically suggests that professionalism is part of a complex of factors operating in different combinations in different situations. The characteristics of professionalism to be analysed in this chapter are themselves related to the particular historical circumstances in which they

95

were generated. The extent to which they can be applied exactly to contemporary occupations is also limited.[4]

Professionalism is but one form of work organisation or orientation to work in society. It both contrasts and overlaps with others. The various features of professionalism can be seen as ranged

DIAGRAM 2

Continua in the Professional Ideal Type

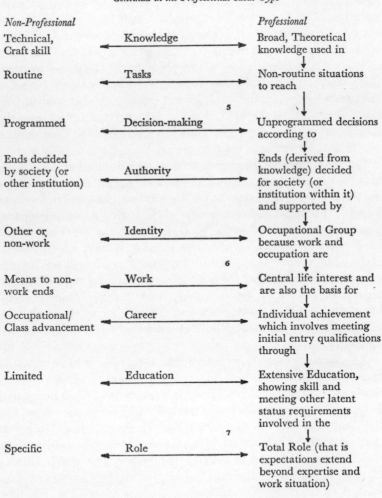

Non-Professional		*Professional*
Technical, Craft skill	Knowledge	Broad, Theoretical knowledge used in
Routine	Tasks	Non-routine situations to reach
Programmed	Decision-making	Unprogrammed decisions according to
Ends decided by society (or other institution)	Authority	Ends (derived from knowledge) decided for society (or institution within it) and supported by
Other or non-work	Identity	Occupational Group because work and occupation are
Means to non-work ends	Work	Central life interest and are also the basis for
Occupational/ Class advancement	Career	Individual achievement which involves meeting initial entry qualifications through
Limited	Education	Extensive Education, showing skill and meeting other latent status requirements involved in the
Specific	Role	Total Role (that is expectations extend beyond expertise and work situation)

96

along a series of continua. These features are usually found together at their most extreme points in the occupations customarily recognised as professions, but they are also relevant to the study of other occupations. These features are summarised in Diagram 2, and will be examined in detail in the course of this chapter. The list is not a complete review of the various characteristics which other authors have included in their different definitions. On the right of the diagram, an attempt has been made to show how these features link together in a self-supporting whole. The diagram includes continua based on behaviour outside as well as inside the work situation. This claim that there are distinctive professional patterns of behaviour outside work itself is particularly important in considering the wider impact of professionalism on society, its relation to other social institutions and the question whether professionals in general constitute a distinct class or status group.

But most of the continua to be discussed in this chapter emphasise the importance of work itself, the skills and knowledge on which it depends and the relationships and organisation which it involves. As we have seen, these have not always been the key features of professionalism. The development of occupational professionalism raises problems at all three levels of analysis distinguished in the introductory chapter. From the point of view of society as a whole we need to investigate the process through which separate specialised occupations have emerged and been granted varying measures of autonomy. This process can also be examined from the point of view of the occupational groups themselves – under what conditions do occupational groups become conscious of their common identity, organise and professionalise? Finally, the focus on work itself raises questions at the individual level, about the nature of professional work and its consequences for a professional social role and life-style. For example, is professional work the contemporary paradigm of non-alienated labour? It is not to be pretended that all these questions can be answered in the space of one short book. The scope for trying out a professional ideal type against empirical studies of professional practice and organisation is itself limited by a lack of such studies, especially in Britain. But it is to be hoped that this analysis will map out the problems, suggest a strategy and point up areas in which further investigation is both necessary and promises to be fruitful.

The attempt to superimpose a professional ideal type on the empirical variety of professional occupations faces various problems of conceptual clarification. One important difference within and between professions is in the variety of different settings in which professionals may practise. The main contrast is between professionals in private practice and those employed by or within various types of organisation. In Chapter 1 we noted that some authors have taken the independence apparently associated with traditional private practice as an archetypal characteristic of a professional occupation.[8] The professional was aspiring to be a gentleman. He could not allow it to be said that he was subordinate to another. Working in organisations has put professionals into the uncomfortable social position of employee and threatened them and their work with a complex of restraints.

On the other hand, it is salutary to consider that among the criteria which Weber specified for his pure type of bureaucracy, the paradigm which has been the foundation stone for much organisation theory, there are several which suggest some overlap with occupational professionalism. For example, Weber specified that candidates should have technical qualifications tested by examination or guaranteed by diploma, that the office should be the sole or primary occupation of the incumbent and that there should be an institutionalised career.[9] The first of these characteristics is especially important when applied to many of the newer 'semi' or 'would-be' professions which have developed through specialisation in industry and commerce.[10]

Weber linked the spread of bureaucracy in society with the switch towards technical certification in education.[11] In the previous chapter it was pointed out that in Britain associations claiming professional status for their specialty have often been the means through which such certification has been introduced. In the process they have also helped to increase differentiation based on technical or functional specialisation within different types of organisation.

Technical certification identifies an occupational group with a specific expertise and makes the group visible beyond the bounds of any particular organisation or social situation.[12] It has often been claimed that professions are occupations characterised by a specialised expertise. But there is a sense in which members of most occupations possess some expertise, however simple the task they perform. Moreover, members of any occupation tend to make the most of whatever expertise a job does involve to increase self-esteem, social status, financial reward or relative power in the work situation.[13] Among the differences between professional expertise and such on-the-job skills is the national, or even international, visibility of the former. This is a necessary but not a sufficient condition for an occupation to be accepted as a profession.

Another distinction commonly recognised between the two types of skills is perhaps more significant in demarcating specifically professional occupations. It is that the expertise should be founded on a theoretical body of knowledge.[14] Nevertheless, visibility is particularly important when considering the claims of occupations working within organisations to be considered as professions. It is a necessary precondition for the development of career structures and occupational orientations outside the confines of a single organisation.

In the course of this chapter it will be argued that organisation is not necessarily the bogyman of professional independence and autonomy as it has generally been cast. Apart from the problems of social status, the essence of the traditional argument has been that there is a necessary conflict between organisational and professional goals and that, within an organisation, the former will dominate and constrict the latter. On the other hand, some of the studies of professional private practice, discussed in detail below, suggest various ways in which independent practice is itself structured by the situation in which it occurs. Some organisations can be seen as insulating professionals from pressures they would face in private practice and providing them with the means to perform their professional tasks in relative security.

Before turning to the detail of specific cases, it is worth reviewing in general terms some of the different characteristics of the two types of practice situation. The contrast set out in the following diagram should be seen in terms of broad tendencies rather than absolute assertions. In some of the professions in which private practice still survives as the dominant employment setting, its characteristics have been changed dramatically by further specialisation and division of labour.

Included in this diagram are the three main reasons why employment within organisations has gradually taken over from private practice as the main professional practice setting. Private practice was predominantly a means through which personal services were provided to personal clients. In some cases practice within organisations has developed because increasing knowledge,

DIAGRAM 3

Differences between Professional Practice in Different Settings

	Private Practice	Organisational	Common
Role	Complex	Concentrated on expertise	Career success leads to positions requiring other component
Practice Goals	Personal/ Corporate Service	Diffuse	Personal/Corporate services requiring technological backing
Client	Own Client Specific Responsibility	Organisation as client/Organisation's Client/No Client (Society) Shared Responsibility	
Career and Individual Goals	Flat Career Pyramid, Achievement through practice	Graded within expertise or movement outside. Individual Achievement	
Salient Reference Groups	Local community	Organisation	Professional community

specialisation and the development of technology has meant individuals can no longer provide the service in isolation. Organisations themselves have a continuing need for a variety of expert services and may employ professionals to provide them. But the oldest reason for the organisation of professional practice is illustrated by such traditional professions as the Church and the Military. In such cases society, not the individual, was the client.

Looking after the spiritual and physical security of the realm were both necessary social functions provided through a frame-

100

work of professional organisation.[15] Recognition that professional goals are not simply individual but social has played some part in the development of organisational structures in other professions, notably medicine. The economic viability of private practice rested on the unspoken assumption that those who needed the service could and would pay for it. The assumption held good while professionals only catered for those who were their social betters or equals. One of the causes of friction within the divided medical profession of the early nineteenth century was the growing realisation that medical need did not respect the traditional economic and status boundaries of medical provision.[16] Just over a century later the National Health Service was introduced embodying the ideal that disease should be treated on the basis of need. The radical shift in perspective involved in treating disease as a problem for society as a whole inspired those who introduced the Service to look forward to a gradual eradication of medical problems from the society.[17]

The legal profession has gone much less far to expand the scope of its clientele. It may be true that because of the nature of the law and the interests and problems it seeks to defend and supervise, the rich still have greater need of a lawyer than the poor. What has certainly been established, by research in America if not Britain, is that the poor have much less opportunity to use a lawyer or the law.[18]

The Components of the Professional Role

The first contrast in Diagram 3 between role complexity in private practice and role concentration within organisations draws attention to the variety of components which may be included within a professional role. Four important components may be distinguished – the performance of the professional services themselves; the development of the knowledge on which such services are based; the communication of this knowledge to professional successors and/or wider publics; and the administration of an employment setting within which such performances can be carried on. Further subdivisions could be made and other components added, especially in such cases as religion or teaching where professional responsibilities are liable to be widely defined

101

and professional tasks overlap with those performed by other occupational groups.[19]

But distinguishing these four components is sufficient to show that they are given different emphasis in different practice settings. To complicate the picture further, they are likely to appear in different combinations at different levels in the same profession or at different stages of the same career. Traditionally the professional in private practice was expected to be omnicompetent, not simply in meeting different demands for his services but also in building a practice, advancing knowledge and training successors. The traditional independent practitioner was much like an entrepreneur marketing his own skill rather than the products of others.[20] His scope for entrepreneurial activity was hedged around by professional restrictions on competition. Processes of change and specialisation within professions have further limited this scope. Similarly the changes in education and training, discussed in the previous chapters, have tended to simplify the role of the private practitioner by taking away the primary responsibility for knowledge and communication.

Such division of labour is endemic in organisations. In them a professional is more likely to be able to concentrate on specifically 'professional' tasks. He is more likely to find his role clearly defined, to be relieved of the problem of finding situations in which to practise and to be provided with the means with which to do it. To follow this line of argument is to make a number of assumptions about the organisation, in particular that there is little conflict or competition between professional and organisational goals. This assumption is questioned by the traditional view of professionals in organisations.

In commercial organisations, for example, professional services will be just another means to financial ends. This may be an oversimplification for many organisations producing products which are evaluated in terms other than cost and in which the management system allows other goals to play a part.[21] Nevertheless, the literature abounds with cautionary tales about the havoc commercial considerations can wreak upon professional standards. One particularly colourful version of this general phenomenon was the Hollywood filmwriters who saw their scripts reworked to fit the commercial beliefs of company executives and vice-presidents.[22] This example illustrates a basic professional dilemma. The company executives controlled the capital and resources through which the writers' work could reach an audience. The executives had to rely on guesswork and proven successes to estimate what the audience would pay to see. Conflict between professionals and executives could be played out as a conflict over who was in a better position to make accurate guesses about the audience. But in this case, as in most others, professionals tended to introduce other considerations, using arguments from artistic creativity and professional integrity. In their most extreme form these arguments suggest professional services can only be supplied according to absolute standards which may be unrecognised by the organisation or its clients.[23]

Those in control of organisations also face a continual dilemma. How best to manage the professional and his work? The professional may prefer freedom to work on his own terms but from the organisation's point of view such terms may not lead in the right direction. Conversely, to attempt to direct and control the work may be both ineffective because of the nature of the work and self-defeating because of the reaction it produces from the worker. Apart from such rational, forward planning considerations, factors of relative status and power are liable to be involved on both sides.[24] Burns and Stalker reported cases in which the leaders of industrial companies, faced with a need for change, were unwilling to accept the implications for their own position that such change might come from research departments.[25] As a result they placed their new research departments off the site and out of mind.

The problem of assimilating professional work within organisations is only a special case of the general problem of incorporating the professions within the general social system. Each profession can claim to have its own set of standards through which decisions in its own field should be reached. The claim is strong in so far as it is backed by one set of means, the professional manpower, and weak in so far as it depends on the supply of other means, such as the resources with which or on which to work.

Etzioni has pointed to the existence of a distinctive professional type of organisation in which means are supplied to achieve such professional ends as the production, application, preservation or communication of knowledge.[26] Professional organisations can be placed on one end of a continuum at the other end of which are organisations which limit and harness professional expertise to the

103

achievement of the organisation's own goals. But any organisation, even a professional one, is liable to develop its own goals according to the conditions in which it is able to survive and grow. To take its place at the professional end of such a continuum an organisation needs to be well insulated from its constituents, those who might be in a position to set the conditions for its survival and growth.[27] In Charles Perrow's terms, 'official' goals are a notoriously unreliable guide to 'operative' goals.[28] The latter depend on the power enjoyed by those representing different interests within the organisation, relative to others both inside and out. Blau, in his study of employment agencies, showed how difficult it was to operationalise some official goals when they conflicted with others of more direct relevance to the way in which the employment agent's own work and prospects were evaluated.[29]

Relationship with the Client

Another difference between private practice and organisations as a setting for professional work is that the latter may provide the individual practitioner with considerable insulation from the client. The ideology of professionalism has always held that the practitioner should have independence and authority when dealing with a client. Payment for a professional service, always a sensitive point, gives no right to question its quality. Clients are expected to know how to act the role of client as the professional expects.[30] Failure to do so may lead to rejection, as in the case of nurse–patient relations studied by Schrober and Ehrlich, or to the professional attempting to teach the appropriate behaviour to the client, as Katz and Eisenstadt found in the unusual circumstances of Israel.[31]

Different types of client may have different conceptions of the client role. Friedson, for example, found that while working-class patients tended to accept their doctor and his methods of treatment uncritically, middle-class patients, especially those with college education, were more critical, more likely to assess the service provided and to 'shop around' for medical services.[32] One compensation for school teachers in Chicago who stayed in low-prestige slum schools was, according to Howard Becker, the fact that they avoided the pressure from middle-class parents to teach their children and help them succeed which was characteristic of suburban milieux.[33] In different practice settings the professional may be exposed to very different pressures. A professional in private practice has to deal directly with these clients and face the problems of finding them, retaining them and securing payment from them. In some circumstances the professional may find himself in a relatively weak position.

The same may also apply to professionals working in organisations when the organisation itself is the client for the service. Others in the organisation may control employment and career opportunities. Moreover, they may not be ignorant about the technical quality of the service. Unlike the individual client they may not only know what they want but also whether it is to be had. Organisation leaders may be ex-professional specialists. Even if they are not, they may have very firm ideas on how the product should be judged, like the film company vice-presidents in Hollywood mentioned above.[34]

The professional is most likely to be insulated from such pressures when he is working in an organisation which supplies services to individual clients; in one which has no clients or in one in which the attributes of the client are divided between different constituents. The first type of organisation, a hospital or a school, takes over responsibility for supplying the clients to the professional, leaving him to perform the service.[35] Such a professional may experience a similar pressure to the private practitioner if the organisation itself is in a weak position *vis-à-vis* clients. If it is not, then conditions may allow the professionals to ignore with impunity the claims of others to question their activities. For example, as in the study by Becker cited above, school teachers may seek autonomy from both formal authorities and the parents of the children they teach.[36] Nevertheless, it remains a question for empirical research whether such professional assertiveness necessarily increases with professional superiority over the client. There may be other intervening factors, such as knowledge and type of practice.

Research institutes provide one of the best examples of organisations in which the functions of the client tend to be divided between different groups. Renée Fox in her study of a hospital research ward has discussed the way in which the doctors had to make decisions between different goals represented by different clients,

105

principally the patients, and the scientific community.[37] Scientists working in a medical research institute had to balance their orientations towards the charity which supported them, the patients and potential patients for whom they worked and the scientific communities of which they were professionally a part.[38] For any individual, the latter were most important in defining career prospects. This meant that most scientists saw their situation as one in which they were able, within broad limits, to follow the dictates of their scientific interests wherever they led. In contrast, they thought the industrial scientist had little scope for choosing his own project or working on it to the full.[39]

This distinction, which has been drawn on the basis of client relationships, cross-cuts another between the practitioner and the researcher, or producer of knowledge.[40] Whereas the former may be found within organisations it is rare for the latter to be found in independent practice. Independent production of knowledge was possible in a pre-professional stage when other sources of income were available aside from an occupation directly supporting the activity. The fact that researchers are mainly to be found working within organisations reverts to the point made earlier that one factor behind organisation is the lack of a specific client. There are various differences between the practitioner and the researcher. Each tends to develop different perspectives and to use different frames of reference for judging and ordering his activities. If the two are called on to work together such differences are likely to create considerable difficulties. For example, practitioners may appear unco-operative in the application of research results or, a special problem in social research, unwilling to co-operate in their production.[41] Researchers may appear too ready to go off at a tangent to follow their own interests and to avoid any problems with practical applications.

The Professional Career

The concept of career is particularly relevant to the professions.[42] It highlights a feature of professionalism common to both types of practice situation. Success is available to individuals on the basis of personal achievement. In this professionals are similar to other members of the middle class. In middle-class employment the

106

individual can hope to achieve wealth, power and status for himself. The working class, on the other hand, can only improve their position by raising the level of the whole class or occupation, or by opting out, in the classic terms of the 'American Dream', into business on their own.[43] Individualism in both professional practice situations can be seen in the twin processes of 'making a name' and 'making a practice'. But there are differences between these two processes. In private practice there is little opportunity for institutional advancement. The practice must be made in the stable context of a local situation. 'Making a name', however, is not a locally oriented process. It is carried out within the national context of the professional association and community.

The overlap between the traditional professions and the ideal of independent practice is underlined by the few opportunities for career advancement which have been available in the older professions. In the past professional career pyramids have been wide at the base and narrow at the apex. This even applies to such traditional professions as the Church and the Military where the profession has been organised within an institutional setting. In the Church of England, for example, there are currently 137 bishops of all types as against 11,330 beneficed clergy.[44] The expectations of most clergy must be even more limited than this ratio of 82 to 1 would suggest. Latent status characteristics have been shown to play an important part in the selection of bishops.[45] Most clergy are in a situation analogous to that of the blocked spiralists identified by Frankenberg in a community setting.[46] They may accept this situation or adapt to it by developing extra-clerical interests as a basis for achievement and prestige.

The flat institutional hierarchies of the older professions have been a source of some difficulty as the professions have been absorbed into organisational practice situations, with unified salary and career structures. Among the current grievances of the junior hospital doctors are the limited opportunities available to achieve consultant status. In school teaching a device has been adopted of creating posts of special responsibility to provide an infrastructure in the teaching career between the basic scale and the headship of a school. Similarly in the universities there is pressure to increase the proportion of professorial positions so that those lower in the hierarchy can have a more realistic expectation of reaching the top. A direct consequence of such a shift would be to

107

lessen the hold which a few men in prestigious and powerful positions can exercise over a profession, its goals and the recruitment of their successors.

But in the previous chapter we noted that the concept of career has been used much more generally in sociology to refer to other changes in an individual's situation and relationships aside from movement through an institutional hierarchy.[47] Different practice situations, although formally at the same level within such a hierarchy, may be accorded very different prestige and status within the profession. This process of internal stratification within professions can be found in both types of practice setting. From the perspective of the professional embarking on a career some settings appear more prestigious than others. They may well offer different opportunities for the performance of different tasks with different types of client.

Where movement within the profession is possible, prestige career routes are likely to develop. Those left in the least prestigious settings will be those without the professional or status characteristics necessary to move. This is not to deny that in some cases a sense of professional vocation may be strong enough to keep a practitioner in a non-prestigious situation, supported by the belief that in a criminal court, a slum school, a psychiatric or geriatric hospital the needs and the opportunities are greater.[48] Nevertheless, the cumulative consequences of lack of prestige, unattractiveness to leaders in the profession and low priority in the allocation of resources may lead to a situation in which practice of the professional skills becomes difficult or impossible.[49] Professional goals may be replaced by others better adapted to the immediate situation. Goals such as keeping the in-patients in or the children quiet leave little room for treatment or teaching.[50]

Orientations and Reference Groups

A most important set of relationships for the private practitioner will be with those potentially in a position to help or hinder him in his attempt to establish and maintain a practice within a local community. These include fellow professionals and other community leaders as well as potential clients. The obverse of this tendency towards a local orientation has been the tendency for a

108

complex of latent status characteristics to attach to membership of the older professions in local communities. Professionals have frequently been evaluated on their own terms, as minor members of the local gentry. Collings, in his study of doctors in general practice immediately after the introduction of the National Health Service, found that this was still the way British doctors were evaluated in rural areas.[51]

While this tendency to treat professionals as representatives of a broad social role rather than a specific occupational one, can still be identified in some circumstances, it has been undermined by various processes of social change. One of these is the change in the nature of community, familiar to students of urban sociology as a shift towards segmented roles and secondary relationships.[52] A second has already been discussed at length. It is the change within professionalism itself from status to occupational professions. A third, which has paralleled the second, has been the gradual change of focus for the professional away from the local community, as practice within organisations has taken over from private practice.[53]

Professional experts working within organisations make up a large proportion of what Musgrove has termed the 'migratory élite'.[54] Their professional and technical qualifications make them visible to a national or even international job market. Geographic mobility among the professional and managerial middle class is a familiar feature of modern society, taking its place alongside such long-established migratory patterns as the drift from country to town. Musgrove links this middle-class mobility to other factors outside change in the professions such as changes in the structure of industry. Locally-recruited business owners (burgesses) have been eclipsed by the managerial executives; family firms by multiple combines.[55]

Another contrast between occupational types which has been based on changes in the style of community is that between the traditional and the 'affluent' worker.[56] Geographic mobility is one of the distinctive features of the 'affluent' worker. Valuing work only as a source of monetary reward, the 'affluent' worker is prepared, so the argument goes, to move if necessary to new locations in search of greater reward. The fact that such workers and organisational professionals both share the characteristic of geographic mobility has contributed one argument to the thesis which

109

Wilensky has summarised as 'the professionalisation of everyone'.[57] In both cases mobility does have important consequences for life-style outside work. Some of these consequences are not dissimilar, as we shall have occasion to remark below. Nevertheless, one clear difference between the two occupational groups has already been hinted at above. That is in their orientation to work.

The contrast which has been drawn between the private practitioner's situation in a local community, as against the potential mobility of an organisational expert within the society as a whole, is a considerable oversimplification. It ignores the fact that membership of a professional association may play an important part in supporting the professional identity of a private practitioner. Similarly the phrase 'local community' covers a variety of different situations ranging from the typically rural squirearchy of status professionalism, through nineteenth-century towns dominated by commercial and industrial élites, to the different systems of relationships and types of community leadership which are to be found in modern urban society.

An example of the shift away from a local orientation occurred during and after the Second World War, when plans for a complete reorganisation of medical practice were under consideration. The B.M.A. was adamant in its preference for national rather than local control over any organised health service.[58] The B.M.A. leadership mainly represented the interests of private practitioners, but on this issue the whole profession was united. One reason Eckstein suggests for the doctors' preference was that as professionals they wanted to avoid contact with local community leaders whom they saw as representatives of commerce and trade. Another reason was the battles between the B.M.A. and the local authorities over the control and conditions of medical practice, which had gone on throughout the whole history of the association.[59]

The contrast is also an oversimplification so far as practice within an organisation is concerned. Professionals within organisations can adopt a variety of possible orientations to the profession, the organisation, the work or the client. These have been spelt out by a variety of authors, using a variety of terms.[60] One factor which makes possible such contrasting orientations is the variety of career routes available within an organisational setting. A basic dichotomy is suggested by the fact that a career may be available either through the profession or the organisation. Gouldner in his

110

study of a college faculty borrowed Merton's terms, cosmopolitan and local, to identify these two types.[61] A cosmopolitan had low loyalty to the employing organisation, high commitment to specialised, professional skills and was oriented to outside reference groups. The locals had the reverse. These two orientations did emerge as polar opposites among the faculty Gouldner studied, but his final categorisation was a little more complicated. Each type included important subgroups. A cosmopolitan, for example, might either be an 'outsider', looking forward to future movement within the profession but through other organisations or he might be an 'empire builder', dedicated to his subject and to his department as a vehicle for that subject, though not necessarily to the organisation as a whole.

Bennis and his colleagues in a study of nurses in an out-patient department found that the cosmopolitan/local distinction did not apply as postulated.[62] Professionalism in the sense of an interest in nursing skills tended to be associated with a local rather than cosmopolitan orientation. To account for this the researchers enumerated various differences between work and career situations of their nurses and those of Gouldner's college faculty. Promotion took a nurse swiftly out of professional nursing service into administrative positions. Professional prestige was only available from the immediate colleague group, fostering a 'local', in-group orientation among the 'professional' nurses. The study underlines two points. First, different career routes are to be found in different professions and organisations, complicating any simple dichotomy. Secondly, one factor contributing to a choice between reference groups will be the perceived significant of allying oneself with such a group and taking on the associated identity in present and future relationships.

Other typologies identifying different orientations among those working within organisations have generally included more than two types. A third orientation, identified both by Reissman in his study of role conceptions among American civil servants and Wilensky in his study of intellectuals in labour unions, is that towards service to the client.[63] The ideology of professionalism would seem to suggest powerful support for such an orientation. Nevertheless, there is a sense in which it is inherently unstable. Only occasionally is the client likely to be treated as a significant reference group. He can rarely exercise any influence on profes-

111

sional career prospects. The ideology of professionalism itself demands that he should not. Such methods for evaluating professional services as are in use have generally been designed specifically to avoid any suspicion that lay opinion might threaten professional authority. There are no direct links between professional service and client satisfaction, not even the market mechanism of the commercial system.

A well-known example of the tenuous connections which exist between the evaluation and performance of professional services is the tendency, predominant in America though not unknown elsewhere, to evaluate the performance of university teachers by the length of their publication list.[64] This example has been given added significance in Great Britain by the recent proposals of the Prices and Incomes Board to introduce student (client) evaluation of teaching performance.[65] The Board recommended that a small proportion of a proposed salary increase should be devoted to merit awards based on this among other methods of evaluation. The Association of University Teachers, doubtless representing the majority of its members, refused to have anything to do with any part of these proposals (except the money).

The Process of Professionalisation

It could be argued that a 'missionary' or 'service' orientation is most likely to be found among the members of an occupation at a fairly early stage in the process of professionalisation. Occupations seeking to establish themselves as professions commonly claim that the service they provide is important, if not vital, to the society. One way in which a profession may first develop as a separate occupational group is when some individuals recognise a social need and become committed to providing for it. These initial pioneers, entering the field from a variety of routes, will be united by their common concern. The development of a new occupational group may open up new career possibilities for others in relatively marginal or terminated career positions, for example those retiring early from the Armed Services. As time goes by and the process of professionalisation continues, qualifications will be laid down for entry to the occupation and entry routes institutionalised. An occupation with pretensions to professional status cannot afford

112

to be seen as a refuge for the unqualified. Good intentions will no longer be enough. More than that, the development of institutionalised career routes within such a profession may make other goals loom larger than good intentions.

Several occupations seem to have followed variations on this natural history of professionalisation. Possible candidates include social work, journalism and, closer to home, sociology itself.[66] One occupation which does not immediately spring to mind is that of the life insurance agent.[67] Nevertheless, Taylor and Pellegrin from their study of this occupation in the United States concluded that the trend towards professionalisation had hindered rather than helped the provision of life insurance services to the community at large. Professionally recruited and oriented agents aimed to find a middle-class clientele of business and professional families. The supply of such business was limited. But rather than extend the scope of their activities down the social scale to tap a ready lower middle-class market, this type of agent preferred to widen his conception of his professional role. He tried to become an agent managing personal estates, not simply life insurance policies. The professionally trained agents also appeared to put considerable emphasis on security and career prospects. Their attitude contrasted with the 'rugged individualism' which many older agents felt had been characteristic of the occupation at an earlier stage. Retrospective images such as this are notoriously unreliable. Nevertheless, the insurance agent appeared to have become more of a desk executive, less of a travelling salesman peddling his wares to members of whatever social strata he could attract.

The process of professionalisation has generally been outlined as a series of stages, marked by changes in the formal structure of an occupation as it aspires to professional status. Wilensky, for example, has outlined five main stages in the professionalisation of occupations in the United States.[68] First, an occupational group must emerge, engaged on full-time work on a particular set of problems. This may be the result of a switch from amateurism to professionalism, such as the process outlined above, or it may follow from the specialisation of knowledge within an existing occupation or through functional specialisation made possible by institutional change. In all cases a new occupational group is likely to have to demarcate its own position and face competition from other overlapping occupations and professions.[69]

113

If it is to continue to develop as a profession such a new occupation must meet certain minimum conditions. One of the most important of these is that it should be non-manual, engaged, in the Webbs' phrase, on 'brain work', or only manual in so far as it is necessary to perform personal services.[70] Professionalisation seems to be more likely in cases where a new occupation already has some connection with an established profession, either through the subdivision of an existing body of knowledge or through working closely with another profession. The social status of the occupation's clientele, if any, and the status of origin of its recruits may also play a part in confirming its claim to professional status.[71]

The remaining stages in the process of professionalisation distinguished by Wilensky can all be seen as attempts by the occupation to secure and stabilise its position in relation to the wider society. The second stage is the establishment of training and selection procedures.[72] This, together with the third stage, the formation of a professional association, is part of a continuing process of establishing and defining the occupational function both to set standards and norms within the occupation and to manage its relationships with other competing groups. These provide the basis for the fourth stage, in which the occupation agitates for public recognition and legal support for its control over entry and modes of practice. Legal support generally takes the form of restrictions on the use of the professional name, though in a few cases direct and indirect restriction have been placed on the performance of the professional function. Finally, Wilensky suggests the occupation will elaborate a formal code of ethics.[73]

Such an outline is a particularly useful way of summarising some of the main characteristics attributed to professions. Nevertheless, it needs to be complemented by an account of the consequences different stages in the process have for the composition of the profession, its activities and goals. The natural history set out above is clearly not the only possibility. It is especially interesting, however, as it suggests that some professions may follow an analogous path to that identified by Weber as the routinisation of charisma. In this process a charismatic leader, the leader of a social movement, is replaced or succeeded by an organisational structure in which his authority and functions are divided and routinised.[74] One consequence is that the initial goals of the leader are likely to be replaced by others, more relevant to the survival

114

of the new institution. Similarly, the process of professionalisation may bring about changes, not only in the formal structure of the occupation, but also in the occupation's means and goals.

Culture and Performance in the Medical Profession

This strategy of investigating the effect different occupational structures and practice settings have on the provision of professional services is one which could be profitably developed in the study of the professions. Enough clues are already available from the literature to suggest there are wide differences which may be substantially related to differences in the practice situation.

In an important paper, Freidson has argued that the private practitioner in the modern American medical and legal professions is liable to become separated from the professional culture to be found in hospitals, medical schools, law firms and law schools.[75] In contrast, he may be exposed to a lay culture with quite different norms and expectations about the practice of medicine or law. Freidson's argument can be extended to show the important consequences different cultural and organisational systems in different professions have for the way the professional services are performed. In different types of practice setting there are different possibilities for gaining a livelihood. Some studies have suggested that in accounting for professional performance, professional ideals, morality and altruism are not entirely without importance.[76] Nevertheless, a general conclusion can be suggested from studies of different professional adaptations in different practice situations. Professional performance develops according to what is perceived to be necessary to achieve the practitioners' goals within the different types of practice structure.[77] These goals may in turn be related to the distribution of prestige and the structure of careers within the profession.

In the early nineteenth century, when the established professions faced concerted pressure for utilitarian reform, defenders of the professions pointed to the exigencies of establishing a practice as the means whereby the competent and fit were sorted from the incompetent and unfit. They argued that special education, training and selection procedures were unnecessary. The unfit did not survive to practise. One consequence of this, pointed out in

115

Chapter 3, was to make it more likely that the fit would be drawn from the ranks of those who had the money to support them and the connections to help them find clients. Such connections might be with existing practitioners, who could help the newcomer by passing on business, or direct with potential clients, the source of such business. In the first case the stage was set for the development of a controlling oligarchy within the local profession able to supervise entry, influence the style of practice and replace itself with new members drawn in its own image.

This was the situation Hall describes in his study of the organisation of medical practice in a small American city.[78] The newly qualified practitioner had to find a clientele and gain access to hospital facilities. In the American medical system this meant ensuring that he was able to provide his clientele with medical services. His colleagues already in the profession controlled access to both these necessities. They could incorporate the newcomer into a career structure based on existing systems of practice and referral in the community.

The colleague group was dominated by what Hall termed the 'inner fraternity' drawn from similar socio-economic and educational backgrounds. This inner core was able to use its power to recreate itself continually in its own image. Newcomers with the appropriate auxiliary status traits, the right ethnic, social and educational backgrounds, were assimilated into the established system. In this particular city there were a few places on the fringe for Jewish, Negro or immigrant practitioners, who did not possess the necessary traits but who were able to draw a clientele from their own ethnic group.[79] In this case the referral system also provided channels of communication and control through which beliefs and appropriate methods of practice and conduct could circulate. In contrast the British system of referral from general practitioner to hospital consultant does not seem to provide the same basis for the development of a common professional culture. Each may lose contact with a case as soon as it is passed to the other.[80] Contact may only be through brief written notes. Above all, the two groups are not linked in any relationship of career dependence. It is a relationship in which neither party has power, though there may be sharp differences in public and professional prestige.

Collings, a general practitioner from New Zealand who under-

116

took an unstructured survey of medical practice in England soon after the introduction of the National Health Service, emphasised the isolated position of the general practitioner in the British medical system.[81] 'There are no real standards for general practice. What the doctor does and how he does it, depends almost wholly on his own conscience.'[82] Collings' survey was heavily criticised by the profession when it was published and must now be decidedly dated. Nevertheless, he used more sociological imagination than is to be found in some later studies which attempted to repair the medical image.[83] He showed, for example, how doctors in both industrial and rural settings seemed to slip into practice routines which were the minimum acceptable to their clientele. He argued that the methods of practice he found in the central city areas, where 'certain routine procedure [were] followed, sometimes almost religiously: throats and tongues [were] looked at, etc.', were a product of the heavy workload, the lack of equipment and facilities and the fact that the practitioner was not integrated or visible within the wider medical profession. Rural doctors, on the other hand, were not subject to the same work pressures. They lived up to a rather different image as longstanding pillars of the local community, 'regarded more or less as "the squire" ' and 'regarded as "good" by both the profession and the public'. The links between this image and the tradition of status professionalism are clear.

A more recent study of patients and general practitioners in Britain suggests that most patients accept their local doctor uncritically.[8*] They do not consider his qualifications, question his methods of practice or realise there may be alternatives. Freidson, in his paradigm of opposition between lay and professional cultures, envisaged the possibility of a lay culture, fully developed, with its own systems of referral and methods of treatment. There is little sign of such a development in Britain, though chemists and others do seem to have played a consultative role in medical matters among the urban working class. Most patients seem only to evaluate their general practitioner for his personal qualities, for the bedside manner hallowed by the tradition of the trade and for his memory. A greeting by name may make them feel like friends or at least individuals rather than anonymous cases.

Cartwright found that from the doctor's point of view the main area of friction was the feeling that they were being overwhelmed with trivial demands. Cartwright shows that this feeling was itself related to the doctor's own security in his professional role. Those who thought a high proportion of their cases were trivial tended to carry out few medical procedures themselves. They did not go on courses for general practitioners and so they had no contact with the clinical sources of the professional culture. They were worried by the apparent decline of general practice. They compared their situation adversely with that of other professionals who appeared secure in their roles. In contrast, those who regarded few of their cases as trivial took another view of the general practitioner's role. They saw themselves not just as dispensers of medicine but also as social and psychological counsellors.

Taking Freidson's dichotomy between professional and lay cultures, the general practitioner in the British medical system seems to occupy a midpoint in which he belongs to neither. Confirmation of this picture must await further research. Such research should include a comparative element to show the effects of different systems of professional organisation on the development of occupational culture and the nature of professional practice. To a limited extent such a comparative perspective can be extracted from the contrast between the accounts of the different medical systems just reviewed. A further dimension can be added by considering studies of the legal profession in the United States. These show, among other things, the way in which some legal practitioners are enmeshed in a set of legal institutions. A separate cultural system develops within these institutions in which law is practised.

Culture and Performance in the Legal Profession

Like the American medical profession, the legal profession in the United States is sharply divided and stratified.[85] This stratification system is based on ethnic and socio-economic differences, perpetuated by different educational experiences. It finds expression in different types of lawyers, doing different legal work in different practice settings. Lawyers in private practice, especially solo lawyers, generally come at the bottom of the stratified system. In Detroit, for example, Ladinsky found that solo lawyers tended to come from minority ethnic or religious groups, from working-class homes, from educational institutions with poor reputations and to

118

have experienced chaotic work histories.[86] Like the doctors outside the hospital-centred professional culture they tended to draw their clientele from their own ethnic group. They mainly worked on non-recurring personal cases such as matrimony, crime and injury for individual clients.

Lawyers working for large law firms, on the other hand, were positively recruited by the organisation.[87] Smigel in his study of the large law firms in New York found that their recruits were predominantly white, male, Anglo-Saxon, Protestant graduates of élite eastern law schools. The law firms went to considerable efforts to recruit this type of graduate, even to the extent of adapting their internal organisation to make it more attractive to potential recruits. These adaptations included giving the new recruit more responsibility and experience and opening career opportunities for him. One aim was to overcome the image of the firm lawyer as the 'kept' lawyer, salaried and controlled by the organisation for which he worked.

The paradox, as Ladinsky points out, is that in spite of the apparent bureaucratisation of the law firms, the so-called independent, solo lawyers were more constricted in several senses by their practice situation. They were unable to widen their clientele, to widen their range of cases and their type of practice, to achieve any visibility or status within the profession. Their functions were constantly threatened by competition with other professionals, such as estate agents and accountants. Above all, they were in a potentially weak position in relation to their clients.

Several studies of American legal practice have attempted to investigate the effects of this relative weakness on the style of practice adopted by the lawyers. Lawyers are liable to be faced with the ethical dilemma of choosing between professional norms and client demands. O'Gorman, in his study of matrimonial lawyers in New York,[88] chose a particularly interesting case for observing such a dilemma. New York matrimonial laws were themselves in disrepute. There were recognised and widely used methods for circumventing the strict letter of the divorce law. The dilemma is precisely summed up in a passage which O'Gorman quoted verbatim from an interview transcript.

If a man is just an ordinary guy and he consults you, you tell him the law and what can be done, and that's the end of it. If

119

the client has a lot of money, its more difficult. You tell him the law, and he doesn't care what the law is. He wants you to do something. That's why he is paying you, and he tells you as much.[89]

The quotation makes it clear that some clients are better able to bring effective pressure than others. This raises the important questions about the distribution of legal services, and by extension the distribution of other professional services, throughout society. We shall return to these in the following chapter.

Carlin, in two studies of legal practice in different American cities, took up this problem of how lawyers in different practice situations experience and resolve such ethical dilemmas.[90] By confronting lawyers with a series of hypothetical ethical dilemmas, Carlin developed an instrument to test their adherence to professional norms. From his findings he suggested that these norms could be divided into three types – Bar norms, accepted by most lawyers throughout the Bar; élite norms, accepted only by the élite lawyers; and paper norms, not accepted by any members of the Bar.

Overall acceptance of norms was strongly related to size and type of practice. The pressure to violate norms was stronger for the low-status lawyers. Ethical violations either took the form already noted of acceding to client demands or they might involve exploitation of the client. Exploitation is possible because the client of the lawyer in solo or partnership practice is likely to be less intelligent than the lawyer, less expert, lacking in social backing and power and, as most low-status legal problems are non-repetitive, unlikely to be a source of further business for the lawyer.

But, as Carlin points out, the rate of violation among solo practitioners was not simply a consequence of the relative power relationship they enjoyed with their clients. The solo practitioner, especially those engaged in criminal practice, may be embedded in a third type of cultural system. This is not professional or lay in the senses distinguished by Freidson but related to the institutions of criminal justice. The lawyer continually works in these alongside members of a variety of other occupational groups associated with law enforcement. Carlin found that 'waiting around' in courts was a good index of exposure to and involvement in the court culture. This contained a set of understandings

120

about how to deal with repetitive problems commonly experienced by those working in the courts.[91] These understandings were not simply at variance with the professional norms but apparently independent of them.

The way in which the court as an organisation system replaces the profession or the client as source of reference and pressure has been clearly stated by Blumberg.[92]

> Organisational goals and discipline impose a set of demands and conditions of practice on the respective professions in the criminal court, to which they respond by abandoning their ideological and professional commitments to the accused client, in the service of those higher claims of the court organisation.

Criminal lawyers need contacts within the court, with the police and the prosecutor's office, for example, to build and maintain their practices. As in the other two cultural systems described above, a referral system plays an important part in maintaining the culture and deciding its content. Blumberg shows that one important consequence of this is that the lawyers and others in the court unite in coercing the client to plead guilty. Lawyers act as 'agent-mediators' helping the accused to take on a new social role of 'guilty man'. The court can then handle its responsibilities easily without threat from such outside bodies as the media, the appellate courts or the political system. The professional and lay stereotype of justice through court-room advocacy, what Wood termed the 'adversary system of justice', is replaced by a system of collusion between the various parties. In this way all can minimise the risks which they face. The lower the status of the court in the American legal system, the closer its relationship to the political system through the election and appointment of officers, the more developed the court culture and the more likely that lawyers regularly practising in them would violate professional norms, even 'Bar' norms.

But before accepting Carlin's conclusion that low-status lawyers are more likely to be tempted and more likely to succumb than high-status lawyers, whose clients are 'primarily large, wealthy corporations and well-to-do individual clients from old American families',[93] it is important to point out that this result may be a product both of the greater visibility of lower-status practice to sociologists and, more specifically, of the distribution of the ethical dilemmas which Carlin used to make up his instrument. These dilemmas seem to be taken more from the experience of the solo lawyer than the firm lawyer. The high-status lawyer has fewer, more regular clients bringing repetitive business. The clients are likely to be of equal educational and social status and, like the wealthy prospective divorcees noted in O'Gorman's study, wise to what can be done, as well as what should be done. Much of the legal business which has developed from the growth of corporate capitalism is outside the traditional set of professional norms associated with the lawyer as an officer of the court, representing individual clients in pursuit of justice. 'The conception of the lawyer now obtaining is that he is a paid servant of his client, justified in using any technical lever that the law supplies in order to forward the latter's interest.'[94] The high-status lawyer is not so much unethical as aethical. This throws further doubt on the attempt to approach the study of professions through norms and ideals, even if the aim is, as Carlin's was, to refute the approach on its own terms.

Carlin's aim was to advance a situational form of explanation which would counter the point of view which 'tends to conceive of professional norms as existing independently of the social and organisational context within which they are meant to operate'.[95] The contrast is the same as that between the situationally specific and the normative view of the professional socialisation process, discussed in the previous chapter. It is possible to be more precise about which features of a given situation will be important in explaining the form and content of professional practice. They will be those which pose problems whose solution is necessary to the achievement of future goals.

In this discussion of different types of private practice we have emphasised different referral systems as one institutionalised system for solving an endemic problem of private practice, that of finding and maintaining a clientele. The referral systems are one basis for the contacts and sanctions necessary for the maintenance of different types of practice culture. Although the marked organisational differences between Britain and the United States must make us beware of transferring substantive conclusions from America to Britain, the general line of approach is one which could profitably be applied to the British professions. The British literature is rich in histories of different professions and discussions of the formal features of professional organisation within them. It is largely empty of studies of professional practice, sensitive to the different forms it takes in different situations.

Discipline, Performance and the Client

Much attention has been given to the problem of the professional–client relationship in theoretical discussions of a professional ideal type.[96] Such discussions have been based on the twin professional ideals that professional authority should dominate the relationship and that the practitioner should use this authority for professional, not personal, ends. Various mechanisms of professional organisation have been taken as attempts to ensure these ideals are met. Pre-eminent are the processes of socialisation, implicit in the lengthy period of education and training and discussed in the previous chapter, and the disciplinary machinery built into the organisation of the profession itself. In the older professions this machinery is backed by such powerful sanctions as disbarment and erasure from the register.

But the impact on the style and content of professional practice depends on the way the disciplinary code is administered and enforced throughout the profession. Carlin noted the low proportion of the New York City Bar who had been arraigned before the disciplinary committees. He questioned whether this was evidence of an overwhelming ethical profession or of weak disciplinary enforcement.[97] The same question could be asked about the disciplinary procedures of English professions. The offences disciplined can be divided into three main types, poor service to clients, breaches of social norms which may involve conduct with clients and attempts at competition or trade practices barred by the profession. The first of these provides the principal public justification for disciplinary machinery; it shows that the profession is in control of its own standards and protecting the public interest. But such offences are a small proportion of even the few offences which reach disciplinary procedures. One reason for this is that the evidence must come from lay clients who are not only ignorant of the professional possibilities but liable to be emotionally involved in their own problems. To accept lay evidence is to

123

threaten professional solidarity based on the profession's control over its own expertise. It also threatens public confidence in the profession's claims to autonomous responsibility. As an eminent American doctor put it, explaining why 'the law is generally with the doctors. . . . To believe in the professional integrity of the doctor is a fundamental tenet of human faith, like the belief in the goodness of mothers, the strength of fathers and Divine Understanding.'[98]

On the other hand, the other two types of offence are likely to be more visible. Offences against social norms may be signalled by the professionals appearing in a court case, charged with drunken driving, or cited as co-respondent in a divorce. Offences against professional norms will produce complaints from other professionals, or again may have taken place in public, as when a professional receives media publicity.

These observations, which are by way of prolegomena to a study of disciplinary procedures in British professions, are based on an analysis of disciplinary cases considered by the General Medical Council during the 1960s. Another important suggestion prompted by this preliminary analysis was that the recognition and prosecution of offences, especially of the second type – those offending social norms – appeared very responsive to changes in the general social climate. Whereas in 1964 the overwhelming majority of all cases considered by the disciplinary committee of the G.M.C. were cases of drunken driving, by 1969 the proportion arraigned for various offences relating to dangerous drugs was as large.

This provides some support for Carlin's conjecture that the main purpose of such disciplinary machinery is not so much to regulate the profession as to present a public front to forestall criticism and any threat of control. To this might be added the function of maintaining restrictions on competition within the profession. This preserves its current structure as a system of stratification and power. A further consequence of the use of the disciplinary machinery as a public front is that those arraigned before it are liable to be cast in the role of scapegoat for the profession. They appear to be drawn from the profession's most marginal members.[99] This reopens the question of the relative rates of incidence of unethical practice in different types of practice situation, already discussed above.

124

Although professional tasks and expertise have been treated as an absolute basis for professional performance from which occasional deviations may be found, it is remarkable in how many professions in modern society there is confusion over the scope and definition of the professional role. Such confusion is often referred to as a crisis.[100] Those professions which still retain private practice seem particularly prone to such crises in which the very existence of the profession, at least as traditionally understood, seems to have been called into question.

One example, already mentioned above, is the 'crisis' in British medical practice. Cartwright's study suggests that doctors are responding to change either by clinging forlornly to their old professional image or by searching for a variety of new ones which would provide them with the security of a demarcated and valuable function. Social and political change have had a similar and paradoxical effect on the Military. At the same time they are responsible for knowing how to fight and for ensuring that they don't have to.[101] Architects have been forced to reconsider their role by technological change in building methods as well as change in the range of possible clientele.[102] One traditional definition, building designer, seems threatened by obsolescence, lack of patronage and encroachment from other occupational groups. One solution is for the architect to cast himself as the leader of a multi-professional team. Another is to cling to the more traditional and narrowly defined role of aesthetic and functional designer.

This contrast illustrates the general point that professional roles are both functionally specific in terms of the particular skills, technologies and intellectual traditions they use and diffuse in terms of their responsibility to provide for social demand and the achievement of broadly-defined professional goals. This is one reason why such crises of confidence are more likely to affect the traditional professions. They have asserted their responsibility for broad social goals. In contrast, the scientific and technological professions have been based more firmly on a specific technology and intellectual tradition.

Religion provides one of the best examples of the way a profession can be pulled in two directions at once. One response to the apparent decline in the demand for religion in modern society has been for the clergyman to emphasise the diffuse responsibility of his role. In this he has been helped by the fact that clerical roles often involved secondary professional functions, springing from the traditional social position of the Church. These functions, such as cultural leader, teacher, medical or social worker, can be moved into a central place by the clergyman, eclipsing his specifically religious responsibilities. The alternative response is fundamentalist, to reassert the clergyman's privileged access to a body of doctrine necessary for the well-being of his clients in society, even though they themselves may refuse to realise it.[103]

This crude contrast begs a variety of questions about the effects of historical changes in religious doctrine as well as the differences to be found between churches and sects differently organised and differently related to their clientele. For example, the contrast between the main organisational forms to be found in Britain and America can be oversimplified as a contrast between private religious practice in America and organisational practice in the principal British churches. In the former there is a tendency for the church and its minister to be the servants of the local congregation on which they are economically dependent. In the latter the professional is to some extent insulated from client and social demand by the organisational superstructure which controls his appointment and career. This is clearly relevant to the argument advanced above against treating organisation as a necessary bogyman for professional practice. The organisation provides the professional with necessary insulation.

Professional Knowledge, Ends and Means

One common theme from these examples of professions in crisis is the attempt to redefine and reassert a basic expertise as the foundation for professional performance. All occupational groups apply or develop particular skills in the course of their work, but in the professions these are based on a more extensive and theoretical body of knowledge which requires more than routine application. William Goode has suggested that the type of knowledge – technical or theoretical – available to an occupation may be an important factor limiting its ability to achieve full professional

126

status.[104] Type of knowledge can be related to the scope and variety of the professional function, and to the structure of control within which the profession operates. Professions with a more substantial and theoretical body of knowledge behind them are better able to convince society of the need for their particular services and perhaps to persuade society of their right to take responsibility for them. Moreover, reference must be made to a theoretical body of knowledge for decisions over ends. In the application of techniques, ends will already have been decided.

The professional's responsibility for interpreting the body of knowledge and for considering, even deciding, upon ends is an important aspect of the autonomy of the individual profession. It introduces an important element of non-routine into the professional's occupation. Both these claims, that professional occupations are non-routine, allowing scope for autonomous judgement, need to be severely qualified by the findings of empirical research, some of which has been discussed above.

Nevertheless, at a theoretical level both are supported by the nature of professional knowledge and the nature of the tasks to which it is applied. Parsons has argued that paradigmatically professionals deal with individual clients at moments of personal or social crisis.[105] By extension it can be suggested that one important function of professions is to manage conflict and crisis within the social system. At the least they are called upon to provide non-routine responses to potentially non-routine situations. In the group of professional occupations supplying services to people, the individual variety of these people and their problems provides the most important source of non-routine situations. In other professional occupations there is a more direct premium on creativity and originality in the work itself, for example in advancing a body of knowledge, creating or performing a new work.[106]

March and Simon in their discussion of the process of routinisation within organisations make a distinction between two types of decision, 'programmed' and 'unprogrammed'.[107] Programmed decisions are those which can be taken by juniors in a hierarchy according to criteria or case law previously laid down. Unprogrammed decisions, however, involve the recognition of a new situation and reference to a hierarchy of ends and goals to fit this situation into accepted practice. Unprogrammed decisions are commonly referred up the hierarchy in an organisation whereas

127

the non-routine, autonomous nature of professions suggests that individual professionals may themselves be expected to take unprogrammed decisions. Such professionals expect autonomy as part of the professional ideal. They may feel thwarted if they find others taking such decisions on their behalf.

March and Simon distinguish a process of routinisation within organisations, whereby unprogrammed decisions are programmed so that they can be taken at a lower level in the hierarchy. An analogous process can be discerned in professional practice. Professionals face the same problems in controlling and ordering work flow and relationships within the context set by their place in the wider society. They need to be able to manage the demands which their work environment places on them. The professional's colleague group, often as represented by the professional association, should provide an important source of reference, guidance and support. But for many practitioners the professional association and other bodies exhorting them to maintain standards may appear quite remote from their everyday experiences.[108] As we have seen, professional and occupational cultures may develop at a variety of different levels, among those working in the same locality, in the same institution, with the same clients though with different responsibilities; wherever there is a group of people able to help each other with useful and acceptable ways of categorising and processing the workload.[109]

Routinisation in March and Simon's sense usually implies greater opportunity for control over work tasks by outsiders other than the practitioners. This is the obverse of the argument advanced above that possession of theoretical knowledge is itself a base of power, however limited. But routinisation can take a slightly different form in which knowledge of the accepted way of doing things becomes itself an esoteric form of knowledge available only to members of the occupational group. Becker has argued that such a tendency is particularly likely in service occupations. Service workers will want to hold those they serve at arm's length to prevent them controlling the work. The jazz musicians Becker studied were artistes as well as service workers and he contrasts the different orientations of those who accepted audience control and went 'commercial' and those who stayed playing jazz, depending on their occupational peer group for standards and support.[110] Reisman has provided an account of ritualisation in legal practice in which legal skills were also developed and used for their own sake rather than in doing a particular job.[111] Again the individual lawyer and his colleagues seem to have been the important audience to witness this performance of professional art. The elevation of technique into art is not confined to artistic performers. As Everett Hughes has suggested, the development of particular languages and skills in a wide variety of occupations, many of which would not be considered as professions, seems to be part of an essentially similar process.[112] The ritualisation of common practice techniques used in common practice situations provides a basis for occupational community and the exclusion of outsiders.

Parsons' pattern variables provide another way of analysing the tensions between routinisation and autonomy.[113] Parsons himself has emphasised the universalistic nature of professional knowledge and skill together with the functional specificity.[114] The ideology of some traditional professions such as medicine and law required that the knowledge be universally applicable and available. Functional specificity, however, suggests a particularistic component in the sense that all problems differ, especially those which individual clients bring to the professional. In such cases the professional may need a great deal of individual knowledge about the client before he can act, 'guilty knowledge' in Everett Hughes' terms. This suggests another sense in which the exercise of professional skills can be seen as an art, emphasising on this occasion the individual diversity of professional practice. Lortie, for example, has pointed to the way in which teaching skill is commonly justified as an individual art, again providing a basis for teacher autonomy in the classroom, the practice situation.[115] Other occupational groups have also stressed the individual skills necessary to perform their work, especially when attempts have been made to introduce routine or standard procedures.[116] Members of most occupations commonly regard sociologists who want to study them with suspicion, for much the same reason. The sociologist seems intent on reducing the variety of individual situations and skills to universal systems and structures.[117] Thus although professional knowledge is universally applicable, it cannot be reduced to a codified expertise, as in Weber's account of the structure of bureaucracy. It includes particularist elements as well. One cause of the crises noted above is that the application of science and technology may turn professional practice into a set of technical routines. If this happens, it poses considerable problems of personal and professional identity for the practitioners in such fields.[118]

Professional Identity

In the course of this chapter one aim has been to develop a dynamic model of professionalism. A complex of factors interact within the professional work situation to pull the practitioners in different directions. One important factor which has been stressed so far is the future orientation of the professional contained in such concepts as career. Another is the meaning which the professional identity has for the individual's self-image. Professional identity is a feature of professionalism common to both independent and organisational practice.

Professional titles mark out practitioners as members of distinct occupational groups associated with the performance of some set of services or tasks. They are relatively specific titles round which definite sets of expectations and simplified stereotypes can develop. In discussing the ethnic stratification of the medical profession in the United States, for example, we commented on the latent status traits associated with doctoring by the public who make up the potential clientele.[119] Such latent status attributes have little to do with the practitioners' professional capabilities. They may provide a means for the professionally ignorant to judge practitioners, based on status considerations taken over from the traditions of the profession or the general status system of the society.

From the professionals' point of view the need to meet various latent status requirements is likely to extend outside working hours. Again this seems particularly apparent in the case of traditional professionals in local community practice. Local clergymen, for example, have a diffuse set of role responsibilities at work which they cannot discard at will. Nor, according to proverb, can the vicar's wife.[120] There are several senses in which the concept of totality, borrowed from Goffman's analysis of institutions involving continuous and complete membership,[121] can be applied to professional roles. The weakest sense of totality in professional roles is that already mentioned above. Most professional roles, at least those of the traditional professions, are generally recognisable

130

by others in society outside any particular work situation. Much of the research which has linked professional and non-professional occupations has dealt with occupations which share with the traditional professions this characteristic of external visibility.[122] The fact that people recognise a particular occupation as uniquely responsible for some area of life,[123] whether it be health or the collection of rubbish, does seem to play a part in creating conditions for a sense of occupational community and identity and in making the practitioner a recognisable social type in the community.

A second sense of totality in professional roles is to be found in the blurred boundary between work and non-work. Formally or informally the members of some professions must always be 'on call', ready to act if they encounter an emergency. Blurred distinctions between work and non-work can, as we shall see, take other forms applicable even in professions in which emergencies are not endemic.

The most powerful sense in which professional roles can be said to be total is in those cases when the practitioner himself is aware that general standards of behaviour or a particular life-style are required of him because of his professional identity and status. Professional disciplinary procedures can define 'infamous conduct' as anything liable to undermine public confidence in the profession, anything which might tempt the public to stop the blank cheque the profession has claimed to freedom of action and responsibility in its particular field. But more important than discipline are the techniques used to specify what type of person is to be accepted as a professional man. The latent status attributes attached to professionals do not simply reflect lay ignorance. They also reflect the profession's need to guarantee itself before society.[124] We have seen in Chapters 2 and 3 that in the guarantee status and character may be as significant as capability. The intermingling of the two traditions of status and occupational professionalism in modern society has important, if confusing, consequences for professional identity.

Professional Ideology

Adopting a professional identity has an impact on thought and behaviour through the development of distinct professional ideologies. The concept of professional ideology which has been developed from the original insights of such authors as Sorokin and Whitehead[125] draws attention in another way to the centrality of work in occupational professionalism and to the development of the national professional community as the focus of professional orientation. Whitehead, for example, was struck by the fact that 'each profession makes progress but it is progress within its own groove . . . the point is the restraint of serious thought within a groove. The remainder of life is treated superficially with the imperfect categories of thought derived from one profession.' An understanding of this phenomenon is crucial to an understanding of the role of professionalism in the division and distribution of knowledge in society. It also raises important questions taken up in the following chapter, about the part which professions can and should play in social policy-making.

Ideology is a concept which has already been overworked in sociology.[126] The excuse for using it to refer to the belief systems of professionals is that other terms, like belief system itself, are unnecessarily clumsy. The use of the term ideology generally implies both that the constituents' beliefs are a selected and possibly distorted version of reality and that they have been prepared for use to justify the group in a situation of possible conflict with outsiders. Some professional ideologies illustrate both these characteristics.

But the term has also been used in the study of professions to refer to belief systems developed within the profession through which the practitioners make sense of their work experiences.[127] This latter type of ideology is related to the occupational cultures identified in the various studies of different occupations carried out by members of the Chicago and 'New Chicago' schools. Such cultures generally included a special occupational slang, norms and standards of work performance, systems for classifying and dealing with repetitive work problems and, in service occupations especially, systems for classifying and maintaining distance from clients. The difference between professional ideologies and occupational cultures is partly one of scale – professional work is more central throughout the individual's life experience – and partly one in kind – professions are generally more concerned about addressing outsiders than other occupational groups.

The study of professional ideologies also borders on problems in

132

the sociology of knowledge. Kuhn, for example, in his study of scientific thought has shown that professional bodies of knowledge cannot be regarded simply as conglomerate accretions of raw facts and theories, ready for indiscriminate use or amendment by the professional.[128] They are already ordered, sorted and interpreted within the theoretical position currently shared within the profession. This theoretical position is likely to entail wider perspectives on the state of society and the world.

One way in which such theoretical positions are maintained is through the professional élites and the control which they can exercise over career opportunities and professional recognition. In Kuhn's terms the structure of a profession helps to keep scientific research within the boundaries of 'normal' science, working on problems set by the current dominant theory. In Whitehead's terms professional work continues in its groove. As is implied by its title, 'The Structure of Scientific Revolutions', much of Kuhn's study is taken up with analysing the occasions when science jumps out of the groove and moves towards a new dominant theoretical perspective. Although there is little space here to go beyond a static account of professional ideology, it is important to remember the possibility of change or of conflict between different perspectives within the same profession. One condition under which such conflict can develop is when the profession itself includes a variety of factions and élites, each controlling access to different institutional career opportunities and sources of professional prestige.

Something of this situation seems to be present in the profession of psychiatry in the United States. This is a profession which is still in the process of establishing itself, demarcating its specific responsibilities and developing a coherent body of knowledge and specific style through which to approach its clients' problems. This profession has served as the main vehicle for studies of professional ideologies, studies in which the researchers have concentrated on explaining the genesis, maintenance and consequence of three conflicting ideologies within the profession.[129] These conflicting ideologies are based on the three contrasting ways through which it is possible to deal with patients' psychiatric problems, by treating them as principally physical, psychological or social. The first two of these three viewpoints appear to be firmly established, recognised as alternatives by psychiatrists themselves and supported by an educational and organisational infrastructure, but Armor and Klerman at least report that the socio-therapeutic ideology is much less well developed. Strauss and his colleagues, using a similar threefold classification, found that differences in ideological position could be attributed to differences in training, in links with the various professional associations and in career experience in different institutions. But they emphasise the interdependence of ideology and situation by showing that professionals were liable to interpret their current institutional experiences in line with the ideology they already held.

Strauss and his colleagues also point out some of the ways in which differences between professional ideologies extend into wider differences in general points of view. Different psychiatric ideologies not only entailed different treatment techniques but also different views on the morality of using different types of treatment and so on the general role and responsibility of the psychiatrist. Because of the claims of professional expertise, professionals tend to justify what they are doing as not only useful, but right. Ideologies include both existential and normative beliefs.

Although it is possible to paint this general picture of professional ideologies, drawing attention to their fourfold basis in the nature of the work, the colleague group, the leadership or professional élite and relationships with outsiders, there is a shortage of empirical evidence on the form which they take in different professions. In particular, closer attention could profitably be devoted to the problem of relating specific ideological content to the structural situations of different professions.

A study of a cancer research institute linked to a hospital revealed a marked difference between the way doctors and scientists interpreted and evaluated cancer research.[130] This difference can crudely be summarised as a contrast between medical particularism, based on the doctors' concern for their patients as individuals, and scientific universalism, reflecting the scientists' interests in the general advance of knowledge. The doctors tended to stress the progress which had been and could be made in cancer treatment by the empirical manipulation of known techniques to suit individual cases. The scientists, on the other hand, generally argued that no progress was possible without advances in basic scientific knowledge. This meant trying to find answers to some of the basic riddles of human life through funda-

134

mental research. These different views show the influence of different patterns of thought based on the nature of the professional task. They were also generated by such factors as the relationship between the two groups in the immediate situation, the particular type of therapy and research carried on in the two institutions and elements of competition between the two groups which derived mainly from the particular history of the development of the research institute.

It was particularly interesting to find in these two closely linked institutions a third ideology, subscribed to by both scientists and doctors. This ideology was oriented much more directly than the other two towards managing relationships with outsiders. The doctors and scientists as well as being members of separate professional groups shared a common occupational identity as workers in the cancer field. Through the work of the cancer charities and the publicity given to cancer research this was a nationally available identity. As cancer workers their role set included various members of the lay public – patients and patients' relatives, workers and organisers in the cancer charities, potential donors to such charities and potential cancer patients. The ideology developed to handle relationships with such groups stressed the advances which had already been made in research and the current scope for treating cancers successfully, given public education and co-operation in coming early to report symptoms. This belief was put forward officially by both institutions. In different ways it was functional for the constituents of both.

This study also provided a convincing answer to those who might argue that there was nothing 'ideological' about this belief – that it was simply a statement of fact, known by professional experience. Members of both groups – doctors and scientists – in their separate professional roles, subscribed to beliefs about matters of fact which were quite at variance with each other and those implied in the 'Early Diagnosis' ideology. For example, they recognised the inadequacy of many diagnostic techniques and the palliative nature of many available treatments. The contrasting ways in which the two groups assessed different types of work in cancer research involved different interpretations of matters of fact. For example, they differed over the history of advances in cancer treatment and research. It must be stressed, however, that these contrasts do not show that one or both groups were wrong,

135

simply that the ideologies which they presented to themselves and their publics were based on selective interpretation of their situation. This selectivity can largely be accounted for by reference to factors in that situation.

To say that beliefs are related to the situation in which they are found is also to imply that they are supportive of it. The use of the concept ideology itself entails a similar view that the ideological beliefs are likely to be self-justificatory. In the cancer hospital and research institute the 'Therapy' ideology of the doctors and the 'Basic Science' ideology of the scientists can be seen as giving support to their different roles. The doctors used empirically developed therapy techniques; the scientists were interested in general scientific problems.

But in some cases the argument has been taken even further by showing how the ideology, and especially the wider perspectives which it entails on the nature of the world and society, are supportive of the institution within which the profession is set. In an early study of a professional ideology, based on published textbooks on social problems and social disorganisation, Mills showed how the different authors shared a common viewpoint focusing on the idea of deviance from established norms and treating deviance as a problem of individual adjustment.[131] As Mills points out, treating it as an individual problem has important implications for social policy and the working of social institutions. A social structural perspective would have quite different implications. Chomsky, in his recent polemic against the 'New Mandarins', has turned the charge against other social scientists.[132] He has argued that their basic approach has been implicitly and explicitly oriented towards the goals and assumptions of the political and business élites who are a necessary source of financial and institutional support. A recent case study of news reporting in the mass media has attempted to make the same point about the professional criteria used by journalists to recognise and interpret 'news'.[133] These are related to the repetitive problems of news reporting within particular occupational and institutional frameworks, which in turn have established a *modus vivendi* with the wider social and political systems. Professional ideas on what should be done, based on their particular knowledge and expertise, should not be regarded as absolute claims but as relative to the profession in question and its place in the social structure. In

136

the final chapter we shall discuss some of the implications of this view for the relationship between professionalism and other sources of authority in society.

The Centrality of Work

These concepts of professional identity and ideology have both emphasised the central importance of the occupational role to the professional. This has also been demonstrated empirically through studies of the life-styles and value orientations of professional workers. Once again the contrast between this account and the pre-industrial situation, described by Marshall, is sharp. The professional was a man of leisure, but now he tends to be a man without leisure. He draws few boundaries between work and non-work activities.

It is a standard postulate of urban and industrial sociology that the various roles an individual plays have been segmented in modern society. In particular work roles and leisure roles have been compartmentalised. Professionals stand out as exceptions to this general process. Most are workers who derive satisfaction from the work itself, not simply from the extrinsic conditions of work or from the rewards it makes available. They are workers whose leisure time and interests tend to be permeated with work or quasi-work activities.[134] Such empirical findings are the obverse of professional norms which stress the professional's interest in work for its own sake. Some professions go further in stressing the need for a vocation if the professional is to be fully involved as well as committed to the professional tasks.[135]

But the question remains whether attachment to work is peculiar to the professions or common to most members of the middle class. Morse and Weiss in a general study of 'The Function and Meaning of Work and the Job' found that both middle-class and working-class men said they would continue work even if they came into sufficient money to stop.[136] But they wanted to do so for different reasons. The middle-class man stressed the interest of their work, the apparent power it gave them over their environment and the satisfaction they got from problem solving. The working-class men, on the other hand, expected to continue working just as an activity to keep them occupied. The middle-class

137

men thought they would continue in the same job, the working-class thought they would set up in business on their own in the hope of gaining more personal freedom.[137]

A more detailed examination of the relationship between specific occupational groups and their work might be expected to show the importance of such factors as the nature of the occupational tasks, the proximity and integration of the professional group and the extent of past educational experience. One might predict that a professional group would be more involved in their work, the closer their contact with fellow professionals within the group, the more intellectual the content of their professional expertise, and the more important this professional expertise itself compared to the other role components.

These predictions are borne out by Gerstl's study comparing university teachers, advertising executives and dentists.[138] *Inter alia* Gerstl found that the university teachers had a greater sense of professional community and greater interpenetration of work and leisure than the dentists. As the dentists were independent practitioners this finding is also relevant to the point made above that different professional identities are apparent in different structural situations. But one study based on only three groups is hardly conclusive, especially as unique geographical factors seem to have helped to build a sense of community at the university. Moreover, Gerstl did not try to disentangle the effect of lengthy educational experience from current occupational situations. As Gerstl himself has pointed out, professionals share many leisure habits in common with a more broadly-defined middle class. Educational attainment has been shown to be an important predictor of different habits and life-styles within this middle class.

Professionalism itself, however, is more central to the contrast between the professional's involvement in his work and the state of alienation, typified for modern industrial man. Marx's idea of work being separated from the worker and set against him by industrial capitalism has been elaborated and schematised, by Blauner among others,[139] to show the various ways in which people can become, or can feel they have become, means rather than ends in the industrial process. Blauner has summarised the four modes of alienation he identified – powerlessness, meaninglessness, isolation and self-estrangement – as reflecting different 'splits' between the worker and his existential experience. Such factors as the central position of work in the professional life-style, the control and autonomy the professional has at work and the importance of work in the professional career suggest that most professionals are not subject to such 'splits' on any of the four dimensions. In particular the individualism inherent in the notion of a professional career plays a large part in allowing the professional to feel he is in control of his destiny.

Empirical Variations on an Ideal Type

In this and earlier chapters we have seen that some sociologists studying the professions have become bemused with form at the expense of substance.[140] One consequence of this has been a pre-occupation with the formal structure and history of various occupations. In turn this has led to a tendency to take the surface at face value. Compared with other fields within sociology there has been an unusual convergence between the writings of some sociologists of the professions and those of some professionals, their subjects. Gouldner's point that sociology in general has become part of popular culture, contributing to society's view of itself, can be applied especially to the sociology of the professions.[141] The work of sociologists, or of those accepted and cited by sociologists, has played an important part in defining and maintaining a professional culture.[142] But it has not been simply a one-way process. Some statements by professionals addressed to a professional audience have been taken over to become part of the basic corpus of the sociology of the professions.[143]

This convergence has encouraged the tendency to accept form as an accurate guide to substance, to take professional ideology on trust. Even when this has not happened directly it may have happened indirectly through the way in which the research problem was chosen and defined. This was one of the main questions raised in the previous chapter about the Columbia studies on the socialisation of medical students.[144] In most cases the research problem was one of effectiveness in implanting professional norms. To simplify the difficulty, a study suggesting no effect does not begin to open up a sociological account of what is happening in that situation. It leaves basic questions about the existence and status of such norms unanswered.

139

In the course of this chapter an attempt has been made to redress the balance in the sociology of the professionals by concentrating on previous work which seems to have direct implications for the substance rather than the form of professional behaviour and relationships. This has meant that some important topics, for example professional association, have received scant attention.[145] Instead attention has been drawn to those studies which show the professional embedded in a dynamic complex of relationships.

This recognition of the dynamic aspect of individual behaviour and relationships has been one of the most significant contributions the sociology of the professions has made to sociological theory as a whole. A simple enumeration of factors cannot be an adequate explanation of any situation until account is taken of the individuals' goals and orientations. This is not to deny the importance of social structural elements in a situation, but to argue, as we have done in this chapter and the last, that those elements are available for use by the individual. Taking a static view, elements like role and culture form part of an interwoven system which appears to be self-supporting and self-maintaining. In a dynamic perspective, however, such elements are no longer immutable. They can be manipulated by the actors in a situation according to their perceptions of their interests. Through concepts such as career the sociology of the professions has underlined the dynamic consequences of change in individual interests and situations. But here again sociology has been responsive to such ideas within the professional ideology as individual advancement.[146] Moreover, this type of change occurs within a bounded situation. The elements for the individual to use are already provided. A clash of interests is necessary to produce some realignment in the rules of the game, taken as a whole.

This discussion of professional practice has suggested that the professional in independent practice may be no more independent or professional than one who works within an organisation. In both cases practice is dependent on the situation in which it takes place as much as on the absolute knowledge and standards of the profession itself. The profession and professionalism is only one factor and orientation present within the practice situation. In organisational practice the career is one of the most important ways of accounting for the relative importance of other factors

140

and orientations. In private practice there is a complementary factor, the need to gain and maintain a clientele.

Earlier in this chapter we discussed a variety of methods used in a variety of occupations and settings to achieve this. These had different consequences for the type of practice culture which developed among the professionals. It is possible to specify a number of alternatives lying between Freidson's two cultural extremes, the professional and the lay. Diagram 4 sets out these

DIAGRAM 4

Type of Culture	Likely Venue	Example
1. Professional	Practitioner dependent on nationally-based professional associations and educational institutions	Freidson's polar case
2. Oligarchic	Practitioner dependent on locally-based professional associations and institutions	Hall on medical practice in U.S.
3. Anomic	Practitioner provided with clientele and independent of other professional or lay groups	Collings, Cartwright on U.K. medical practice
4. Collaborative	Practitioner dependent on others outside profession	Blumberg, Carlin and Wood on U.S. criminal law practice
5. Lay	Practitioner dependent on clientele with own norms and expectations of practice	Freidson's polar case

various cultures and provides a counterpart to the more usual typology of role orientations within organisational practice.[147] The examples of each culture discussed in this chapter are set out in the right-hand column. In each culture a different group, with a different set of interests, is dominant. The hypothesis is that professional practice varies between the different cultures according to what is necessary to meet these interests. But there may be considerable overlap in any given situation. Criss-crossing career routes in the past and future or other roles made available by other groups within a situation may all play a part in diverting an individual's orientation from the simple pattern hypothesised

141

Diagrams 3[148] and 4 both show that the scope for realising the various features of professional practice set out in the continua of Diagram 2[149] varies considerably between different practice settings. This has been a continuing theme of this chapter. There is a continual tension between ideal and reality in any account of professions and professionals.[150] Indeed, perhaps one of the most distinctive features of professionals is that they have such an ideal available to them.

Paradoxical consequences proliferate from this tension. Merton's comment, that for each professional norm there is an opposite, was quoted in the previous chapter. It is echoed by a conclusion which could be drawn from this chapter that quite opposite forms of behaviour may both gain the label 'professional'. The professional is a responsible, autonomous individual, and yet at the same time the professional is the one who is sufficiently integrated into a situation to recognise the cues and know the routine responses. This process of routinisation is implicit in the discussion of different practice culture or role orientations. In the process varying weight is given to the occupation and the knowledge on which it is based. But this is the key feature of professionalism which accounts for its usefulness in different situations as an ideal and role model. It provides a measure of insulation from other role groups – employer, client, society at large – which can be bought by emphasising knowledge and occupation. To say professional autonomy depends on insulation is simply the other way of looking at it. In work and non-work situations, professions are occupations writ large.

5 The Professions in Society

The professions have always occupied a marginal position in society, peripheral to the main divisions of class, status, power and interest. This is still the case even though the professions have changed from being an addendum to the nobility and gentry to being part of the occupational élite in modern society. Change in the position of the professions has been contingent on changes in the society around them. The aristocracy's traditional claim to power and status has lapsed in favour of the utilitarian claims of the industrial, commercial and political élites. Among such élites the professions stand out as a group whose members share common socio-economic origins, educational experiences and life-styles and a common, if confused, ideology of professionalism. In contrast, other contemporary élites, though they may be more closely linked internally through such traditional mechanisms as kinship ties, tend not to appear as such a unified group.[1] The professions have benefited from the process whereby occupation has become the main basis of differentiation in modern society. They appear to fill the vacuum in mass society,[2] but this appearance can be challenged both on the grounds that they do not constitute a conscious, coherent élite group and that their grasp on power and rewards in society is limited and insecure.

The professions are divided among themselves by subject, tradition and status. Different types of training, association and employment situation are to be found between and within different professions. The individualism of the professional career acts as a divisive force within each profession. The continuing decline of private practice may have the effect of removing one of the basic divisions within and between professions, but it remains to be seen whether common experience of employee status will change the basic values of professionalism.

Professionalism itself has rested on a series of contradictions. One of these has been the contrast between individualism and the defence of common interests through guild-like organisation. A second is reflected in the difference between status and occupational professionalism, or, in training, between vocational and non-vocational education. In Britain this has been compounded by the association between the aristocracy and the traditional professions. This connection gave rise to a third contradiction, the attempt to present professionalism as an alternative to capitalist economic philosophy when growth in the professions was dependent on that same economic system. The professional is also liable to be torn between meeting the narrow requirements of doing a professional job and following the wider implications of the profession's world view.

At a more practical level there are such contradictions as that between the élitist basis of professional service and universalistic assumptions about its applicability, a contradiction that is expressed in different ways in different professional–client relationships. Another practical difficulty is that of reconciling individualism and creativity at work with the routinisation following from professional norms and standards. This book has been mainly concerned with these contradictions and paradoxes of professionalism as a contrast to the more usual functionalist approach which has stressed the integration of professions and society. To a large extent professionalism is a cultural phenomenon.

Underlying these various contradictions is the fundamental problem of the professions, that they lack self-sufficiency. Professionalism is the ideology of occupations moving towards such a goal. The goal is differently applicable at the three levels, society, occupation and individual, distinguished in the first chapter of this book. Some occupations have moved closer to it than others at different points. But in all cases the pursuit of this goal is a pursuit of occupational power and this cannot be expanded indefinitely. Occupational power rests on knowledge and organisation. But whatever the aspirations of different professions, professional knowledge is not a self-sufficient basis for decisions on future courses of action and professional organisation cannot by itself secure the means for professional work.

Originally means were provided through the professional's familial wealth and connections, or directly by the client. In the first case the professional was expected to conform to a leisured life-style with little relevance to professional practice. The second case has involved a variety of pressures on the form and content of professional work and a variety of attempts by professionals to insulate themselves from them. Some of these are illustrated by contemporary studies of professionals in private practice. These have also illustrated some of the problems involved in distributing professional services to those unable to supply the means. Differences are liable to develop in the kind and quantity of the service made available to different sections of the population. One claim for professionalism is that it provides the individual client receiving a personal service with a guarantee of quality. As professions have developed serving corporate clients, such a guarantee has become less necessary for the client and more relevant to society as a whole. Society has an interest in controlling the ways in which such corporate clients achieve their ends. It has also developed an interest in the standard of service supplied to individual clients. In Britain legal regulation or the provision of services through government agencies has provided an important spur to professional organisation, in particular to the development of occupational interest groups.

The problem of distributing professional services, the changing morality of professionalism, increasing State intervention and the decline of private practice are all interrelated. Some occupations which do not have clients in the individual sense have espoused professionalism, or at least tried to make the most of their specialised expertise. Widening the definition of the client has been one accepted way of countering attempts by the recipient of the service to have a say in the way it is provided. Some professions, particularly those producing knowledge, can claim to have no client, except society in a very general sense. This introduces a new set of problems about professional–client relationships. The claim of such occupations to be able to represent the social good themselves is inherent in the ideology of professionalism. Dispute centres on the legitimacy of this claim and on the alternative claims of other groups and organisations, especially those providing the means for research, to act as agents for the social interest. Changes in the way resources are provided for professional work have introduced new problems and new competitors for the professions in pursuit of occupational power.

Contemporary difficulties in financing medical services highlight the problems which remain when the State has taken over

145

responsibility for financing personal services without following through the full implications of society rather than the individual being the client. Under the National Health Service the State has undertaken to pick up patients' bills as a means of introducing an equitable distribution of costs and services. The development of medical science and technology is fast making this an open-ended commitment. The fact that this form of commitment should have been undertaken without question is a greater tribute to the institutional power and importance of the medical profession than the survival of the private sector in medicine. The contrast between private and public sources of finance is less significant than the contrast between curative and preventive medicine, the former based on the provision of services by professional practitioners to individual clients, the latter on meeting social needs through social action.

Similar contradictions can also be found outside medicine and the public sector among professionals working for private industry and commerce. There has been much dispute recently as to whether the managers of large-scale corporate organisations still follow the creed of profit maximisation.[3] But even the criteria suggested as alternatives, for example the continued growth of the corporation, leave little room for professional standards of quality and service or the concern with a variety of reference groups implicit in professionalism. A minor indication of the marginality of professionalism is the tendency for it to be relegated to disregarded isolation within an organisation for reasons of tradition or prestige. But while this is possible in such cases as research and development, other specialised financial or legal services have to be more closely tuned to the organisation's needs. The scope for the development of independent professional standards is correspondingly lower. This would seem to be one reason for the lack of interest such professions show in theoretical knowledge or academic learning, whatever academic definitions of a profession may have laid down as necessary for professional status.

In assessing a profession's attempts to achieve occupational power it is important to differentiate between the direct defence of the interests of members of the occupation and wider attempts to define the nature and scope of the occupation's activities in society. These wider attempts may have implications for the

146

immediate interests of practising professionals, as for example was suggested above in the contrast between curative and preventive medicine. Nevertheless, they have traditionally been considered more legitimate as an aim of professional organisation and association than the direct defence of interests.

The professions' main competitors in their attempts to define their own ends and means are the State and profit-making organisations. These are the two mechanisms which have taken over from the individual client or familial connections as the main sources of means for professional activities. Both use criteria for allocating resources and evaluating future courses of action which are fundamentally different from those of professionalism. Economic authority rests on judgements of what can be manufactured and supplied profitably within the existing framework of economic institutions. Political authority similarly rests on judgements of what is practical and desirable, given the wishes and interests expressed through the political system.

Professional authority, on the other hand, appears to be more absolute. The profession claims unique responsibility for some aspect of the public good. It also claims to know how that good should be achieved. A simple illustration of the contrast between political and professional authority has occurred in local government in the choice between administration by elected councils or expert managers.[4] One advantage of a manager is that he can take the long-term view without the short-term fear of losing favour. In a sense he can choose from a wider range of options than those which would normally be considered practical politics. But such a system not only raises the short-term problem that the immediate wishes of the people may be frustrated. In the long run there is the problem of control endemic to any system of paternalist dictatorship or, in the case of professionalism, paternal élitism. Professional élitism, the suggestion that judgement about ends could be made according to professional criteria by those with the requisite knowledge, is one reason for the ideological alliance between the professions and the aristocracy.

But there are distinct difficulties in extending professional absolutism beyond the immediate concerns of its own field of interest. Within the field a judgement may appear absolute, but no way is available to resolve the conflicting aims of different fields or to decide the allocation of scarce resources between fields. The

147

difficulty is even more fundamental, however. It can be argued, as we saw in the previous chapter, that absolute claims within a field are not simply based on the potential of available knowledge, but on that potential set within the particular socio-economic situation of the profession and its practitioners. The situation of the professions under the Fascist régime in Germany provides the most striking evidence both for the narrowness of professional concerns and the mutability of professional knowledge, standards and opinion.[5] Fascism has often been considered as the apotheosis of irrationality in a political system and yet one of its initial attractions seems to have been that it offered the prospect of political decisions being taken on the grounds of absolute social good rather than according to the whim of democratic political machinery. The machinery of the Fascist State isolated and subordinated each professional group within this absolutist framework so that professionals could only pursue their own concerns within their own field.

Professionalism is at the same time outward and inward looking, even under quite different political systems. Within the physical and biological sciences, for example, there has been a continual difference between those content to confine their attention to immediate problems within science and those who have argued that the scientist should take part in decisions on the application and use of scientific results. The scientist has a more difficult task than the doctor or the lawyer in convincing others that he has any special authority to pronounce on the use of science. His general responsibility to advance knowledge is more obviously open to qualification by other goals than a general responsibility for health or justice.

These characteristics of professional specialisation and authority are one reason for the fact that the professions, while they constitute an occupation élite in modern society, have only limited access to and control over power. Professionalisation and specialisation of function and task have not affected those in the upper echelons in society who exercise political and economic control so much as the broader section of the population immediately below them. To call the controlling group an élite is to beg the question of whether it shows sufficient cohesion and consciousness of common purposes. It does, however, appear to be characterised less by specialisation than by the diversity of the different roles its members fill and by

148

the variety of cross-cutting links binding it together. It is only a slight exaggeration to argue that a professional will come closer to centres of power and influence the more he relinquishes his specific professional function. As we have seen, such a process is built into the professional career as the professional role widens to include administrative and other duties.

These speculations on the place of professions in modern society are based less on an attempt to understand how they fit, to elucidate their structural-functional position, than to examine some of the contradictions and paradoxes of their present situation. The ubiquitous phenomenon of professions in crisis in itself suggests that a dynamic perspective tracing the combination of divergent factors which have led up to the present situation is more likely to be fruitful than an approach which starts simply from the characteristics of that situation. It also invites speculation about the possible course of future developments. It seems likely that this will depend on the relative weight given to the three types of authority, economic, political and professional, and the extent to which conflict between them becomes explicit instead of remaining, as it has in the past, suppressed. This in turn will depend on the extent to which contemporary economic and political systems continue to be viable, a question which takes us far beyond the scope of a study in the sociology of the professions.

Professionalism, we have argued, is not viable by itself but it plays an important role as a countervailing source of rhetoric and criteria for action. The contradictions within it and its absolutist pretensions means that it could play such a subordinate role within other types of political and economic systems. It might also play a part in a process of social change leading to the establishment of a different system. Without a breakdown in the various mechanisms which integrate the professional into an acceptable status position in contemporary society, such a possibility appears remote.

Pre-eminent among such mechanisms is the individualism involved in the professional career. The shift from independent practice to employee status might be expected to reduce the scope for the pursuit of individual careers and to develop a consciousness of common interests. Given the current social position of the professions and the history and traditions of professionalism, the

149

attempt to assert professional authority and criteria against the conflicting considerations of politics and economics is likely to continue.

Such mechanisms as the control of entry, qualification and pricing policies, while directed explicitly to such ends, have also had implicit consequences in maintaining professional status and rewards.[6] The direct defence of occupational interests may become more explicitly a matter of concern to professional associations. In some cases this has already happened. The changing employment situation in the professions appears to be undermining the professional's claim to be able to express his interests differently from those of other workers.

'Crisis' seems to be particularly endemic in the traditional professions.[7] In the course of this book we have traced the various implications of the change from status to occupational professionalism. The most fundamental threat has been to the exercise of the specific professional function. In different cases the precise nature of this function has become ambiguous, or been overtaken by technical change or the development of new specialisms and new knowledge. Professional organisation is suited to social change at the general level, in the sense that through professionalisation new occupational groups can emerge demarcating newly emergent functions. What is more difficult, however, is to bring about change within a given profession. The patterns of thought and activity which develop within a profession are supported internally and externally by its own structure and the relationship it has established with other organisations and associations. Not only career and economic interests are at stake, but also established patterns of thought and ways of approaching the world.

The shift from status to occupational professionalism has also helped to bring about a 'crisis' in the traditional professions by undermining some of their established claims to social prestige. On the one hand, the social distribution of the clientele for various professional services has widened; on the other, there has been an apparent widening in the recruitment of professional practitioners. Universalistic criteria, based on achievement, have apparently replaced particularistic, ascribed characteristics though, as noted in Chapter 3, the evidence for such a change in actual recruitment and selection is far from convincing. The education system itself is in transition between a status and occupational system account-

150

ing for the current complexity of educational organisation. To some extent the problem of dealing with low-status clientele has been handled by stratification within and between different professions. It remains to be seen whether such devices will be adequate to maintain the social position of the professions in the face of continuing social change.

The attempts made by a variety of occupations to use the name 'profession' as a claim to appropriate status and rewards have also been a threat to the standing of the traditional professions. The members of such professions in the traditional practice settings still enjoy noticeably higher incomes than those in salaried employment. But it remains to be seen how long this will continue, if only because of the trend away from independent practice. During this century an increasing number of women have been recruited into a variety of professions. At the same time levels of income and prestige have fallen, though it has yet to be established which, if either, is the causative factor in this process.[8] In some ways the growth in the number of professions and professionals has undermined rather than strengthened the claim of the professional group as a whole to its position in society.

Previous chapters have underlined the value of a dynamic perspective in the sociology of the professions. This was particularly useful in resolving the difference between ideational and situational ways of explaining individual behaviour in both training and practice situations. The individual in such situations forms and uses a social identity based on his past experience, present situation and future aspirations. Thus combined, these three factors contributed to an explanation of action and belief.

A dynamic perspective is also relevant to wider questions about social rather than individual change. In this chapter we have traced some of the issues surrounding the future of professionalism in modern society. Many of these issues are unresolved. For a variety of reasons the professions have an insecure hold on their place in society so that we may question the future of the professions as a distinct status élite and the future of professionalism as a hybrid ideology. On the other hand, the main strength of the professions, the feature which seems most characteristic in contemporary society, is their ability to exploit their particular expertise, the criteria and standards it involves, to counter the control of other groups and the claims of rival ideologies. The contradictions and ambiguities surrounding the concepts of profession and professionalism make projection difficult, but they help to make the sociology of the professions an intriguing field of study.

Notes

1 Introduction

1. Routh, G., 'Occupation and Pay in Britain 1906–60 (Cambridge, 1965); U.S. Bureau of the Census, 'Statistical Abstract of the United States 1966', 87th ed. (Washington, D.C., 1966).
2. Marshall, T. H., 'The Recent History of Professionalism in Relation to Social Structure and Policy', in 'Canadian Journal of Economics and Political Science', vol. 5 (1939).
3. Weber, M., 'The Theory of Social and Economic Organisation' (London, 1964).
4. For a recent discussion, see Nichols, T., 'Ownership, Control and Ideology' (London, 1969).
5. Habenstein, R. W., 'A Critique of "Profession" as a Sociological Category', in 'Sociological Quarterly', 4 (1963) 291–300.
6. This strategy has been particularly fruitful in the work of Hughes and his students. Hughes, E. C., 'Men and their Work' (Glencoe, 1958). See also Berger, P., 'The Human Shape of Work' (London, 1964) and the section on the world of work in a recent volume of papers presented to Everett C. Hughes, 'Institutions and the Person', ed. Becker, H. S., Geer, B., Riesman, D., Weiss, R. S. (Chicago, 1968).
7. Cogan, M. L., 'The Problem of Defining a Profession', in 'The Annals of American Academy of Political and Social Science', 297 (1955), 105–11. Cogan's first attempt may be found in 'Toward a Definition of Profession', in 'Harvard Educational Review', 21 (1953) 33–50.
8. Hughes, op. cit. (1958) pp. 44 ff.
9. Ibid, ch. 2 and ch. 11.
10. Habenstein (1963).
11. As, for example, in the analysis of self-rated class. See Runciman, W. G., 'Relative Deprivation and Social Justice' (London, 1966).
12. Weber (1964) p. 110.
13. Millerson, G., 'The Qualifying Associations' (London, 1964), Table 1–1, p. 5.
14. The Monopolies Commission, 'A Report on . . . Restrictive Practices . . . in the Supply of Professional Services', Cmnd. 4463 (London, 1970), pp. 5–6. See also Appendix 5. Another variation can be found in Lee Taylor's survey of 'Occupational Sociology' (London, 1969).
15. Hickson, D. J. and Thomas, M. W., 'Professionalisation in Britain : A Preliminary Measurement', in 'Sociology', 3 (1969), 37–54.
16. Carr-Saunders, A. M. and Wilson, P. A., 'The Professions' (London, 1933).
17. Durkheim, E., 'The Division of Labour in Society' (London, 1964).
18. Quoted by Henry Pelling in 'A History of British Trade Unionism' (Harmondsworth, 1963) p. 202.
19. Rothblatt, S., 'The Revolution Among the Dons, Cambridge and Society in Victorian England' (London, 1968).
20. Carr-Saunders and Wilson (1933) p. 499.

21. See, for example, MacIver, R., 'The Social Significance of Professional Ethics', in 'The Annals of the American Academy of Political and Social Science', 297 (1955) 118–24. This paper was first published in the Annals in 1922.

22. Tawney, R. H., 'The Acquisitive Society' (London, 1961; first published 1921).

23. Parsons, T., 'The Professions and the Social Structure', in 'Social Forces', 17 (1939) 457–67.

24. Parsons, T., 'Remarks on Education and the Professions', in 'International Journal of Ethics', 47 (1937) 365.

25. For Parsons' view that an assumption of economic self-interest is not necessary to economics, see 'The Motivation of Economic Activities', in 'Essays in Sociological Theory', revised ed. (Glencoe, Ill., 1954).

26. See, for example, Timasheff's paper on 'Business and the Professions in Liberal, Fascist and Communist Society', in 'American Journal of Sociology', 45 (1940) 863–9. This paper builds on the argument of Parsons, op. cit. (1939). Sections of both are reprinted consecutively in Vollmer, H. M. and Mills, D. L., 'Professionalisation' (Englewood Cliffs, N.J., 1966) pp. 55–61. Another example of the shift in emphasis with a more avowedly polemical purpose is Lewis, R. and Maude A., 'Professional People' (London, 1952).

27. See especially 'Social Structure and Dynamic Process: The Case of Modern Medical Practice', in Parsons, T., 'The Social System' (Glencoe, 1951) ch. x.

28. Sorokin, P., 'Society, Culture and Personality' (New York, 1947), especially the section on 'The Differentiation of Occupational Groups', pp. 211–15; Whitehead, A. N., 'The Adventure of Ideas' (Harmondsworth, 1942).

29. For references to particular studies, see the discussion of this topic below, pp. 131–7.

30. Goode, W. J., 'Community Within a Community, The Professions', in 'American Sociological Review', vol. 22 (1957).

31. Apart from Parsons and Goode in works already cited, Merton has been influential in developing this approach as summarised in the rest of the paragraph. See Merton, R. K., Reader, G. G. and Kendall, P. L. (eds.), 'The Student Physician' (Cambridge, Mass., 1957) and the Columbia University Seminar on the Professions (mimeo; 1952).

2 The Development of the Professions in Britain

1. Saltz, A., 'Occupations: Theory and History', reprinted in 'Man, Work and Society', ed. Nosow, S. and Form, W. H. (New York, 1962) pp. 58–62.

2. As, for example, Reiss, A. J. jr., 'Occupations and Social Status' (Glencoe, Ill., 1961), Hall, J. R. and Jones, D. C., 'The Social Grading of Occupations', in 'B.J.S.', vol. i (1950).

3. Harrison, W., 'Description of Britain', in Raphael Holinshed, 'Chronicles of England', 1st ed. (1577). Quoted in Laslett, P., 'The World We Have Lost' (London, 1965) p. 34.

4. Coxon reports this as a common response from clergy and ordinands he

studied. Coxon, A. P. M., 'A Sociological Study of the Social Recruitment and Selection of Anglican Ordinands', Unpublished Ph.D. Thesis, Leeds, 1965.

5. On the universities at this time, see Rashdall, H., 'The Medieval Universities', ed. Powicke, F. M. and Emden, A. B., 3 vols (Oxford, 1936) and Armytage, W. H. C., 'The Civic Universities' (London, 1954).

6. The description is Rashdall's and Carr-Saunders' and Wilson's, op. cit. (1933). Their work is still the most comprehensive source on the history of the professions.

7. Rashdall (1936) vol. 3 p. 446.

8. Gretton, R. H., 'The English Middle Class' (London, 1917).

9. Tropp, A., 'The School Teacher' (London, 1957).

10. Carr-Saunders and Wilson (1933) p. 67.

11. Laslett (1965).

12. Marshall, T. H., 'The Recent History of Professionalism in Relation to the Social Structure and Policy', in 'Canadian Journal of Economics and Political Science', vol. 5 (1939).

13. Ibid., p. 325.

14. Pirenne, H., 'Guilds', in 'Encyclopaedia of the Social Sciences', vol. 7 (New York, 1949) pp. 208–14. Reprinted in part in Noscow and Form (1962). See also Pirenne, H., 'Medieval Cities' (Princeton, 1925).

15. See above, pp. 6–9.

16. On this point see especially Lewis R. and Maude A., 'Professional People' (London, 1952).

17. Reader, W. J., 'Professional Men' (London, 1966).

18. Hughes suggests patronage was especially difficult to exercise in the Army, even for those with powerful political influence. Hughes, E., 'The Professions in the Eighteenth Century', in 'Durham University Journal', vol. 8 (1952).

19. Otley, C. B., 'The Origins and Recruitment of the British Army Élite, 1870–1959', Unpublished Ph.D. Thesis, Hull, 1965 (a).

20. For general discussions of this problem, with special reference to American experience, see Huntington, S. P., 'The Soldier and the State' (Cambridge, Mass., 1957), and 'Power, Expertise and the Military Profession', in Lynn (1963).

21. Elias, N., 'Studies in the Genesis of the Naval Profession', 'B.J.S.', vol. i (1950).

22. Newman, C., 'The Evolution of Medical Education in the 19th Century' (London, 1957).

23. See Jones, C. and Jenkins, H., 'The Social Class of Cambridge University, Alumni of the 18th and 19th Centuries', in 'B.J.S.', vol. i (1950).

24. Armytage (1954) p. 133.

25. Laslett (1965).

26. Halevy, E., 'Imperialism and the Rise of Labour' (London, 1951) p. 331.

27. Quoted by Carr-Saunders and Wilson, op. cit. (1933) p. 38.

28. For some modern comments on this, see Erskine, N. I., 'The Selection of Judges in England', in Honnold, J. (ed.), 'The Life of the Law' (Glencoe, Ill., 1964).

29. Quoted by Armytage (1954) p. 57

30. Quoted by Coxon (1965) p. 122.

31. Reader (1966) p. 47.

32. Quoted by Newman (1957) p. 8.

33. See especially Hughes (1952).

34. This section on change in the medical profession is based on a number

of sources which will not be cited specifically except for direct quotations. The reader is referred to them for further information on what is perhaps one of the best documented historical processes of change in the professions. Carr-Saunders and Wilson (1933); Holt-Smith, B., 'The Medical Profession in the 18th Century', in 'Economic History Review', iv (1951) 141–69; Hughes, E. (1952); Holloway, S. W. F., 'Medical Education in England, 1830–1858 : A Sociological Analysis', in 'History', xlix (1964) 299–324; Newman (1957); Reader (1966).

35. Carr-Saunders and Wilson (1933).
36. Holloway (1964) p. 301.
37. Stevens, R., 'Medical Practice in Modern England' (London, 1966) p. 18.
38. Holt-Smith (1952).
39. Carr-Saunders and Wilson (1933).
40. Holloway (1964).
41. Quoted by Vaughan, P., 'Doctors' Commons' (London, 1959) p. 36.
42. Apart from Carr-Saunders and Wilson (1933) and Reader (1966) the main source on the history of the legal profession is Abel-Smith, B. and Stevens, R., 'Lawyers and the Courts' (London, 1967).
43. Kaye, B., 'The Development of the Architectural Profession in Britain' (London, 1960).
44. Millerson (1964).
45. Halsey, A. H., 'British Universities', in 'Archives Europeénes de Sociologies', 3 (1962) 85–101; see also Jobling, R. G., 'Some Sociological Aspects of University Development in England', in 'Sociological Review', 17 (1969) 11–26.
46. Halevy (1951).
47. Quoted by Reader (1966) p. 97.
48. Otley, C. B., 'The Army as a Profession', Unpublished Paper read at a Research Seminar, University of Manchester, 1965(b).
49. Otley (1965(a)); Razzell, P. E., 'The Social Origins of Officers in the Indian and British Home Armies, 1758–1962', in 'B.J.S.', vol. 13 (1963).
50. Quoted by Otley (1965(a)), p. 113.
51. This report is taken as the starting-point of Michael Young's fable of our time, 'The Rise of the Meritocracy' (London, 1958).
52. Kelsall, R. K., 'Higher Civil Servants in Britain' (London, 1954).
53. Armytage (1954).
54. Wilkinson, R. H., 'The Gentleman Ideal and the Maintenance of a Political Élite', in 'Sociology of Education', vol. 37 (1963–64).
55. See, for example, Anthony Sampson's strictures against amateurism in 'The Anatomy of Britain Today' (London, 1968).
56. Gerth, H. H. and Mills, C. W., 'From Max Weber – Essays in Sociology' (London, 1948) pp. 426–34.
57. See Reader (1966) and Kelsall (1954), who discusses at length the problem of 'smatterers' who had passed through the crammers.
58. Rothblatt, S., 'The Revolution of the Dons' (London, 1968).
59. Jones and Jenkins (1950).
60. Quoted in Rothblatt (1968) pp. 133–4.
61. Again see Jobling (1969) and Halsey (1962).
62. Jones and Jenkins (1950).
63. Guttsman, W. L., 'The Changing Social Structure of the British Political Élites, 1886–1935', in 'B.J.S.', vol. 2 (1951); 'Aristocracy and the Middle Class in the British Political Élite', in 'B.J.S.', vol. 5 (1954); 'The English Political Élite' (London, 1963).

156

64. Bamford, T. W., 'Public Schools and Social Class, 1801–1850', in 'B.J.S.', vol. 12 (1961).
65. Kelsall (1954). On university recruitment from public schools, see his (post-war) study, 'Applicants for Admissions to Universities', in 'Report of a Committee of Vice-Chancellors and Principals' (1957).
66. Gross, J., 'The Rise and Fall of the Man of Letters' (London, 1970).
67. Again see Millerson (1964).
68. See especially Kaye's explanation of professional organisation in architecture (1960).

3   Selection, Recruitment, Education and Training

1. For the United States, see Reiss, A. J. jr. (1961); for Great Britain, Hall, J. and Jones, D. C., 'The Social Grading of Occupations', in 'B.J.S.', vol. 1 (1950).
2. Blau, P. M. and Duncan, O. D., 'The American Occupational Structure' (New York, 1967).
3. The data on British professional earnings which follows are taken from Routh (1965). More up-to-date information on earnings in a variety of specific professions is available from the reports of a number of statutory bodies, including 'The Review Body on Doctors' and Dentists' Remuneration' and the 'National Board for Prices and Incomes'.
4. The British group of 'higher' professionals includes several occupational groups paid directly or indirectly from public funds. In general, professional self-employment is more common and more resilient to changing trends in the organisation of employment in the United States than in Britain.
5. Millerson (1964).
6. Routh (1965).
7. Ben-David, J., 'Professions in the Class System of Present Day Society', in 'Current Sociology', vol. 12 (1963–64).
8. But see Routh (1965) p. 12 for a careful set of national comparisons.
9. Ben-David (1963–64).
10. Marx, K., 'The Eighteenth Brumaire of Louis Napoleon', in 'Selected Works', vol. i (London, 1962).
11. Weber (1964).
12. On social mobility and educational selection the two seminal books are Glass, D. V. (ed.), 'Social Mobility in Britain' (London, 1953); Floud, J., Halsey, A. H. and Martin, F. M., 'Social Class and Educational Opportunity' (London, 1958).
13. For contrasting views on the development of higher and further education, see 'Report of a Committee on Higher Education' (The Robbins Report) (H.M.S.O., London, 1963) and Robinson, E. E., 'The New Polytechnics: The Peoples' Universities' (Harmondsworth, 1968).
14. See Floud, J. and Halsey, A. H., 'English Secondary Schools and the Supply of Labour', in Floud, J., Halsey, A. H., Anderson, C., 'Education, Economy and Society' (Glencoe, 1961).
15. Clarke, B. R., 'The Open Door College' (New York, 1960); see also Berelson, B., 'Graduate Education in the U.S.A.' (New York, 1960).
16. Reisman, D. and Jencks, C., 'The Viability of the American College',

in Sanford, N. (ed.), 'The American College' (New York, 1962); Jencks, C. and Reisman, D., 'The Academic Revolution' (New York, 1968).

17. Self-recruitment is the tendency for an occupation to 'recruit itself' from the sons of present members.

18. Blau and Duncan (1967).

19. Kelsall, R. K., 'Applicants for Admissions to Universities', Report of a Committee of Vice-Chancellors and Principals (1957).

20. 'Report of the Royal Commission on Medical Education (Todd Commission)', Cmnd 3569 (London, 1968) Appendix 19.

21. Coxon (1965).

22. Kelsall (1957).

23. Kuiper's data on 'The Recruitment of the Learned Professions in the Netherlands' present a similar picture for that country. 'Transactions of the 3rd World Congress of Sociology' (London, 1956) pp. 230–8.

24. Quoted by Cotgove, S., in 'Education and Occupation', in 'B.J.S.', vol. 13 (1962).

25. The Registrar General's classifications of social classes 1 and 2 comprise higher professional, managerial and other professional occupations.

26. 'Report of the Committee to consider the Future Numbers of Medical Practitioners and the Appropriate Intake of Medical Students' (Willink Committee) (London, 1957).

27. Kessel, R. A., 'Price Discrimination in Medicine', in 'Journal of Law and Economics', vol. i (1958).

28. The crucial selection stage was entry to a secondary school. Thereafter students tended to follow separate channels. See, *inter alia*, papers in Floud, Halsey and Anderson (eds.) (1961). Cotgove, S. F., 'Technical Education and Social Change' (London, 1958). See also the surveys conducted for the Robbins Committee (1963), and the 'Crowther Report' – 'Report of the Central Advisory Council for Education, "15–18" ', 2 vols. (London, 1960).

29. Robbins Committee (1963) Appendix 2B. The associations were the Royal Institute of Chartered Surveyors, the Institute of Chartered Accountants in England and Wales, the Chartered Institute of Secretaries and the Law Society. The proportions leaving school before the age of 18 were R.I.C.S. 74 per cent; I.C.A.E.W. 64 per cent; C.I.S. 82 per cent and L.S. 41 per cent. The proportion attending independent or direct grant schools was (respectively) 31 per cent, 50 per cent, 30 per cent and 63 per cent.

30. Gerstl, J. E. and Hulton, S. P., 'The Engineers: The Anatomy of a Profession' (London, 1966).

31. Perkins, H., 'Key Profession' (London, 1969).

32. Ibid., p. 240.

33. Jackson, B. and Marsden, D., 'Education and the Working Class' rev. ed. (Harmondsworth, 1966).

34. Ibid., p. 179.

35. Ibid., pp. 105–6.

36. Ibid., p. 132.

37. Ibid., p. 113.

38. Ibid., p. 161.

39. Rosenberg, M., 'Occupations and Values' (Glencoe, 1957).

40. Ginzberg, E., Ginsberg, S., Axelrod, S. and Herma, J. L., 'Occupational Choice: Towards a General Theory' (New York, 1951).

41. Beardslee, D. C. and O'Dowd, D. D., 'Students and the Occupational World', in Sanford (ed.) (1962).

42. Ibid., p. 610.
43. Becker, H. S. and Carper, J., 'The Development of Identification with an Occupation', in 'American Journal of Sociology', vol. 61 (1956); 'The Elements of Identification with an Occupation', in 'American Sociological Review', vol. 21 (1956).
44. Rogoff, N., 'The Decision to Study Medicine', in Merton, R. K., Reader, G. G. and Kendall, P. L. (eds.), 'Student Physician' (Cambridge, Mass., 1957). See also Thielens, W. jr., 'Some Comparisons of Entrants to Medical and Law School', in the same volume.
45. Kandell, D. B., 'The Career Decisions of Medical Students', Unpublished Ph.D. Thesis, Columbia University, New York, 1960.
46. Coxon (1965).
47. Katz, F. E. and Martin, H. W., 'Career Choice Processes', in 'Social Forces', vol. 41 (1962). The paper reports a study of career choice among nurses.
48. Clements, R. V., 'The Choice of Careers by School Children' (Manchester, 1958) p. 15.
49. Becker, H. S., 'Notes on the Concept of Commitment', in 'AJS', vol. 65 (1960).
50. See, for example, Jackson, B. and Marsden, D. (1966) or Willmott, P., 'Adolescent Boys in East London' (London, 1966).
51. It is the focus on symmetry and equilibrium in role theory which seems to have given weight to such criticisms as that of Wrong, D., in 'The Oversocialised Conception of Man', in 'ASR', vol. 26 (1961).
52. Goode (1957).
53. Becker, H. S., Geer, B., Hughes, E. C. and Strauss, A., 'Boys in White' (London, 1961); Merton, Reader and Kendall (eds.) (1957). These two studies are referred to as the Kansas and Columbia studies respectively.
54. Becker et al. (1961) pp. 46–7.
55. Goffman, E., 'Encounters' (New York, 1961) p. 85.
56. Goffman, E., 'Asylums' (New York, 1961).
57. Ward, R. H., 'A Critical Comment on the Applicability of Goffman's Concept of the Total Institution', Unpublished Dissertation for the Diploma for Advanced Studies, University of Manchester, 1964.
58. In particular, see Etzioni, A., 'A Comparative Analysis of Complex Organisations' (Glencoe, 1961); Wheeler, S., 'The Structure of Formally Organised Socialisation Settings', in Brim, O. G. jr. and Wheeler, S., 'Socialisation after Childhood' (London, 1966). Bidwell, C. E. and Vreeland, R., 'College Education and Moral Orientations: An Organisational Approach', Unpublished Paper presented at American Sociological Association Annual Conference, 1962. The same authors have applied their typology in a study of the 'houses' at Harvard University. 'Organisational Effects on Student Attitudes: A Study of the Harvard Houses', in 'Sociology of Education', vol. 38 (1965). There are some terminological differences between the two papers.
59. Fichter, J. M., 'Religion as an Occupation' (New York, 1961).
60. See below Chapter 4, pp. 130–1.
61. Masland, J. W. and Radway, L. I., 'Soldiers and Scholars: Military Education and National Policy' (Princeton, 1957).
62. Janowitz, M., 'The Professional Soldier' (Glencoe, 1960). See also Anon, 'The Making of the Infantryman', in 'AJS', vol. 57 (1946).
63. Dornsbuch, S. M., 'The Military Academy as an Assimilating Institution', in 'SF', vol. 33 (1954–55). Neither the Coast Guard Service nor its Academy have such long traditions as the senior services in the

United States, but the Academy was modelled directly on West Point and Annapolis, the two longest established training institutions serving the Army and Navy respectively. For a study of West Point Cadets, see Lovell, J. P., 'The Professional Socialisation of the West Point Cadet', in Janowitz, M., 'The New Military' (New York, 1964). The contrast between Lovell's study and that of Dornsbuch almost exactly parallels the contrast in aims, methods and perspectives between the two medical studies discussed below.

64. These terms are taken from Wallace, W. D., 'Institutional and Life-Cycle Socialisation of College Freshmen', in 'AJS', vol. 70 (1964–65).

65. On degradation processes apart from Goffman, E. (1961), see also Garfinkel, H., 'Conditions of Successful Degradation Ceremonies', in 'AJS', 61 (1956) pp. 420–4.

66. Implicitly from Dornsbuch's data it seems that there was a heavy drop-out rate in the first year. Institutions of professional education may continue the processes of selection and recruitment discussed in the previous chapter by 'cooling out' those who do not meet the requirements or lack sufficient commitment.

67. Bidwell and Vreeland (1962).

68. Merton *et al.* (eds.) (1957) pp. 40–1.

69. Christie, R. and Merton, R. K., 'Proceedings for the Sociological Study of the Values Climate of Medical Schools', in Gee, H. H. and Glaser, R. J. (eds.), 'The Ecology of the Medical Student' (Assoc. of American Medical Colleges, Evanston, Ill., 1958).

70. Becker *et al.* (eds.) (1961) p. 34.

71. Becker *et al.* (eds.) (1961) p. 431.

72. In addition to Becker *et al.* (eds.) (1961) see Becker, H. S. and Geer B., 'The Fate of Idealism in Medical School', in 'ASR', vol. 3 (1958); Psathas, G., 'The Fate of Idealism in Nursing School', in 'Journal of Health and Social Behaviour', vol. 9 (1968).

73. Lortie, D. C., 'Laymen to Lawmen, Law School and Professional Socialisation', in 'Harvard Educational Review', vol. 29 (1959).

74. Mauksh, H. O., 'Becoming a Nurse', in 'Annals of the American Academy of Political and Social Sciences', vol. 346 (1963); Shuval, J. T., 'Perceived Role Components of Nursing in Israel', in 'ASR', vol. 20 (1963).

75. See above, pp. 74–5.

76. On the stratification of the American Bar, see Chapter 4, pp. 118–23.

77. Hill, K. R., 'Medical Education at the Crossroads', in 'British Medical Journal', vol. 1 (1966) – quotation from p. 971. Since Professor Hill made these comments some attempts have been made, mainly under the auspices of the Royal College of General Practitioners, to introduce a component of training for general practice into the medical course in British hospitals, but these do not invalidate the general point.

78. Wheeler (1966).

79. Coxon (1965), especially Chapter 5.

80. Strictly speaking, the first of these was not a theological college but a pre-theological college hostel in which ordinands either studied to enter the theological college proper or from which they attended university courses.

81. Huntington, M. J., 'The Development of a Professional Self-Image', in Merton *et al.* (eds.) (1957).

82. It must be pointed out that there were important differences between the medical school studied in the Kansas research and those which

were the subjects of the Columbia studies. The Kansas school recruited from its local community and aimed to produce doctors for that community, most of whom would go into general practice. The Columbia schools were situated in metropolitan centres on the American east coast. They were involved in various educational and training experiments, particularly to bring students into closer and earlier contact with patients, and one aim of the research was to evaluate these. Bloom has suggested that these differences largely explain the different results obtained in the two studies, but while they may account for such limited discrepancies as whether or not students were able to think of themselves as doctors, they do not seem to remove the basic theoretical contrasts between the two studies. See Bloom, S. W., 'The Process of Becoming a Physician', in 'Annals of the American Academy of Political and Social Science', vol. 346 (1963).

83. Box, S. and Ford, J., 'Commitment to Science: A Solution to Student Marginality?' in 'Sociology', vol. i (1967); see also Cotgrove, S. and Box, S., 'Science, Industry and Society' (London, 1970).
84. Merton (1957) pp. 77–8.
85. Christie and Merton (1958).
86. For another discussion of these different approaches, see Becker and Geer's (1958) criticisms of the work of Eron, L., e.g. 'The Effect of Medical Education on Student Attitudes: A Follow-up Study', in Gee and Glaser (eds.) (1958), 'The Effect of Medical Education on Medical Students', in 'Journal of Medical Education', vol. x (1955).
87. On this point, see Halloran, J. D., 'The Social Effects of Mass Communications', in Halloran, J. D. (ed.), 'The Effects of Mass Communications' (London, 1970).
88. Merton (1957) p. 70, original emphasis.
89. Brim, O. G. jr., 'Socialisation Through the Life Cycle', in Brim, O. G. jr. and Wheeler, S. (1966).
90. Zald, M. N., 'Organisational Control Structures in Five Correctional Institutions', in Etzioni, A. (ed.), 'Readings on Modern Organisations' (Englewood Cliffs, 1969); Wheeler, S., 'Socialisation in Correctional Communities', in 'ASR', 26 (1961) pp. 699–712.

4   Professional Practice

1. Pre-eminently Tawney (1961), Carr-Saunders and Wilson (1933) in their section on 'Professionalism and the Society of the Future', and Marshall (1939).
2. Marshall's paper takes off from a rebuttal of Laski, H., 'The Decline of the Professions', in 'Harpers' Monthly Magazine' (Nov., 1935) pp. 656–7. See also Sidney and Beatrice Webb, 'Special Supplement on Professional Associations', in 'New Statesman', 21 April, 1917; Mills, C. W., 'White Collar: The American Middle Classes' (New York, 1956).
3. To take three of the main characteristics which appear in the work of Talcott Parsons (1951).
4. In other words, classification and categorisation in sociology is unlike such processes in the natural and biological sciences. Reductionism, for example, cannot be employed to understand structural wholes. This

makes the cultural relativism of concepts and categories appear more of a problem, but it can also be seen as strengthening the analysis by adding an awareness of that extra dimension.

5. These terms are taken from March, J. G. and Simon, H. A., 'Organisations' (New York, 1958). Like the others in this diagram, they are explained subsequently in the course of the chapter.

6. 'The Idea of Work as a Central Life Interest of Professionals' is the title of a paper by Orzack, L. H., in 'Social Problems', vol. 7 (1959). He was applying a concept taken from Dubin, R., 'The Industrial Workers' World: A Study of the Central Life Interests of Industrial Workers', in 'SP', vol. 3 (1956).

7. The term 'total role' is an adaptation from Goffman's concept of total institution, Goffman (1961).

8. As, for example, Lewis and Maude (1952).

9. Weber (1947) pp. 333–4. See also pp. 413–15. Albrow in his recent account of Weber's theory uses the term 'professional' instead of 'technical' in reporting the first of the criteria. Albrow, M., 'Bureaucracy' (London, 1970) p. 44. Others have also written of the twin processes of bureaucratisation and professionalisation as if they were essentially similar. See, for example, Wilensky, H. L., 'Intellectuals in Labour Unions' (Glencoe, 1956).

10. Various attempts have been made to differentiate between professions using such labels as 'established', 'semi' and 'would-be'. See Carr-Saunders, A. M., 'Metropolitan Conditions and Traditional Professional Relationships', in Fisher, R. M. (ed.), 'The Metropolis in Modern Life' (New York, 1955); Reiss, A. J. jr., 'Occupational Mobility of Professional Workers', in 'American Sociological Review', vol. 20 (1955).

11. Weber (1948) pp. 240 ff.

12. See especially Prandy, K., 'Professional People: Scientists and Technologists' (London, 1965).

13. For a case in point see Crozier's account of the behaviour of maintenance engineers in 'The Bureaucratic Phenomenon' (London, 1964).

14. Carr-Saunders took the difference between an established body of theoretical knowledge and codified technical skills as a criterion for differentiating between 'established' and 'semi' or 'would-be' professions. Carr-Saunders (1955); Goode reaches a similar conclusion in 'The Theoretical Limits of Professionalisation', in Etzioni, A. (ed.), 'The Semi-Professions and their Organisations' (New York, 1969).

15. As the Church has lost its pre-eminent social position there has been a continuing tendency to redefine religion as an individual rather than a social issue. This suggestion has an interesting bearing on Coxon's thesis that the ministry is moving against the tide, that it is a deprofessionalising occupation. Coxon (1965).

16. See Chapter 2 above.

17. In the Beveridge Report one of the main justifications for a National Health Service was that it would reduce the cost of the National Insurance Scheme proposed. 'Social Insurance and Allied Services', Report by Sir W. Beveridge, Cmnd. 6404 (H.M.S.O., 1942) pp. 158–63. For some comments on why this particular aspiration proved overoptimistic see the following chapter.

18. See, for example, Carlin, J. E. and Howard, J., 'Legal Representation and Class Justice', in 'UCLA Law Review', 12 (1965) 381–437; Conard, A. F., Morgan, J. N. and Pratt, R. W. jr., 'Automobile Accident Costs and Payments' (Ann Arbor, 1964). For a paper taking a

162

different view, see Mayhew, L. and Reiss, A. J. jr., 'The Social Organisation of Legal Contracts', in 'American Journal of Sociology', vol. 34 (1969).

19. A point emphasised especially in Fichter (1961).

20. See especially Mills (1956).

21. This has been suggested as a possible consequence of introducing the salaried manager as a new occupational group into industry between worker and owner. On the general process, see Bendix, R., 'Work and Authority in Industry' (New York, 1956); for a discussion of some problems of goal definition and displacement, Charles Perrow, 'The Analysis of Goals in Complex Organisations', in 'AJS', 26 (1961) 854–65.

22. Some of the best accounts are fictional and autobiographical, e.g. Schulberg, Bud, 'What Makes Sammy Run?' (London, 1967, paperback ed.); Miller, M. and Rhodes, E., 'Only You, Dick Daring' (New York, 1964). See also Powdermaker, H., 'Hollywood: The Dream Factory' (Boston, 1950) and Coser, L., 'Men of Ideas' (New York, 1965).

23. For a general discussion of the problem in the mass communication process, see Philip Elliott, 'The Making of a Television Series: A Case Study in the Sociology of Culture' (Constables, 1972).

24. See especially Wilensky's account of the role of the hospital administrator in comparison to other professional administrators and in relation to the powerful and prestigious physician: 'The Dynamics of Professionalism: The Case of Hospital Administration', in 'Hospital Administration', 7 (1962) 6–24.

25. Burns, T. and Stalker, G. M., 'The Management of Innovation' (London, 1961).

26. Etzioni, A., 'Modern Organisations' (Englewood Cliffs, N.J., 1964).

27. See Philip Selznick, 'Foundations of the Theory of Organisation', in 'ASR', vol. 13 (1948).

28. See Perrow (1961).

29. Blau, P. M., 'The Dynamics of Bureaucracy' (Chicago, 1955).

30. Parsons (1951) includes an analysis of the role of sick person.

31. Schrober, D. and Ehrlich, D., 'Rejection by Mental Health Professionals; a Possible Consequence of not Seeking Appropriate Help for Emotional Disorders', in 'Journal of Health and Social Behaviour', 9 (1968) 222–32; Katz, E. and Eisenstadt, S. N., 'Bureaucracy and its Clientele – A Case Study', reprinted in Etzioni, A. (ed.), 'Readings on Modern Organisations' (New York, 1969).

32. Freidson, Eliot, 'Patients' Views of Medical Practice' (New York, 1961).

33. Becker, Howard S., 'The Career of the Chicago Public School Teacher', in 'AJS', 58 (1952).

34. See note 22 above.

35. For a case in point, see Strauss, A. L., Schatzman, W., Bucher, R., Ehrlich, D. and Sabshin, M., 'Psychiatric Ideologies and Institutions' (London, 1964).

36. Becker, H. S. (1952), 'The Teacher in the Authority System of the Public School', in 'Journal of Educational Sociology', vol. 27 (1953). See also Lortie, D. C., 'The Balance of Control and Autonomy in Elementary School Teaching', in Etzioni (ed.) (1969).

37. Fox, R. C., 'Experiment Perilous' (Glencoe, Ill., 1959).

38. Elliott, Philip, 'Men Against Cancer and the Men and Women Against

Cancer in a Research Institute and Cancer Hospital'. Centre for Mass Communication Research, University of Leicester, 1971 (mimeo).

39. For a general survey of these and related problems, see Kornhauser, W., 'Scientists in Industry' (Berkeley, 1962).

40. In Everett Hughes' typology of occupations the term 'profession' is reserved for the former, 'science' for the latter: Hughes (1958). For a further discussion of this distinction, see Freidson, E., 'The Impurity of Professional Authority', in Becker *et al.* (eds.) (1968).

41. For a case in point, the relationship between media researchers and broadcasters, see 'Proceedings of International Seminar on Broadcaster/ Researcher Co-operation', Centre for Mass Communication Research, University of Leicester (1971).

42. Reference was made in the previous chapter, pp. 74–6, to sociological use of the concept in the study of professional socialisation.

43. Chinoy, Eli, 'Automobile Workers and the American Dream' (New York, 1955). The corollary of this, as pointed out by Prandy, is that professions and their associations are status phenomena – they provide the framework within which members can succeed, trade unions within the working class are class phenomena – they represent the interests of the workers in an occupation taken as a whole. Prandy (1965).

44. 'Whittaker's Almanack' (1970 ed.).

45. Morgan, D. H. J., 'The Social and Educational Backgrounds of Anglican Bishops—Continuities and Changes', in 'B.J.S.', vol. xx (1969). The concept of latent status was used by Gouldner, A., in 'Cosmopolitans and Locals – Latent Social Roles', in 'Administrative Science Quarterly', vol. 3 (two papers) and was further discussed by Becker, H. S. and Geer, B., 'Latent Culture – A Note on the Theory of Latent Social Roles', in 'Administrative Science Quarterly', vol. 5.

46. Frankenberg followed Watson in applying the term 'spiralist' to socially and geographically mobile members of the 'new middle class'. 'Blocked spiralists' are those who have 'reached their highest and farthest point'. Frankenberg, R., 'Communities in Britain' (Harmondsworth, 1966); Watson, W., 'Social Mobility and Social Class in Industrial Communities', in Gluckman, M. and Devons, E. (eds.), 'Closed Systems and Open Minds' (Edinburgh, 1963).

47. See especially Becker and Strauss (1956), Becker (1964), Goffman (1961).

48. See, *inter alia*, Becker (1952 and 1953); Wood, A. L., 'The Criminal Lawyer' (New Haven, Conn., 1967).

49. Two examples from British experience are primary schools – 'Children and their Primary Schools (The Plowden Report)', 2 vols. (London, 1967), and mental hospitals, Morris, P., 'Put Away: A Sociological Study of Institutions for the Mentally Retarded' (London, 1969).

50. On schools and hospitals the work of Becker and Goffman, previously cited, is relevant. For a discussion of some aspects of the problem in relation to 'correctional institutions', see Zald (1962).

51. Collings, J. S., 'General Practice in England Today', in 'Lancet', 25/3/54, p. 555.

52. Again see Frankenberg (1966).

53. In Watson's terms fewer professionals can be 'burgesses', most are likely to be 'spiralists'. For a recent discussion of spiralism, see Edgell, S., 'Spiralits: Their Careers and Family Lives', 'BJS', vol. xxi (1970). See also Bell, Colin, 'Middle Class Families' (London, 1968).

164

54. Musgrove, F., 'The Migratory Élite' (London, 1963).
55. In addition to Bendix (1956) see Burnham, J., 'The Managerial Revolution' (Harmondsworth, 1945); Dahrendorf, R., 'Class and Class Conflict in Industrial Society' (London, 1959); Nichols (1969).
56. Pre-eminently the work of Goldthorpe, Lockwood, Beckhoffer and Platt. For a survey and references, see Mackenzie, G., Review Article: 'The Class Situation of Manual Workers: The United States and Britain', in 'BJS', vol. xxi (1970).
57. Wilensky, H. L., 'The Professionalisation of Everyone', in 'AJS', vol. 70 (1964); mobility was one of the common features identified by Foote, N., 'The Professionalisation of Labour in Detroit', in 'AJS', 53 (1953) 371–80.
58. Eckstein, H., 'Pressure Group Politics' (London, 1960); 'The Politics of the British Medical Association', reprinted in Rose, R. (ed.), 'Studies in British Politics' (London, 1969).
59. See also Vaughan (1959), Stevens (1966).
60. Initially Reissman proposed subdividing the general category, bureaucrat. Reissman, L., 'The Study of Role Conceptions in a Bureaucracy', in 'SF', vol. 27 (1949). Other categorisations can be found in Wilensky (1956), Gouldner (1958).
61. Gouldner (1958).
62. Bennis, W. G. et al., 'Reference Groups and Loyalties among Nurses in an Outpatient Department', in 'Administrative Science Quarterly', vol. 3 (1958).
63. Reissman (1949), Wilensky (1956).
64. Wilson, L., 'The Academic Man' (New York, 1942); Caplow, T. and McGee, R. J., 'The Academic Marketplace' (New York, 1958); Jencks and Reisman (1968).
65. 'Pay of University Teachers in G.B.: First Report' (National Board for Prices and Incomes, London, 1969).
66. Wilensky (1956) discussed the instability of the idealistic missionary orientation for individuals in a given occupational situation. Alvin Gouldner, sketching out a sociology of sociology, has emphasised the dramatic effects which the profess of professionalisation had on the type of knowledge produced within the discipline: Gouldner, A., 'The Coming Crisis of Western Sociology' (London, 1970).
67. Taylor, M. L. and Pellegrin, R. J., 'Professionalisation: Its Functions and Disfunctions for the Life Insurance Occupations', in 'SF', vol. 38 (1959–60).
68. Wilensky (1962 and 1964).
69. See, for example, Goode, W. J., 'Encroachment, Charlatanism and the Emerging Profession', in 'ASR', vol. 25 (1960).
70. Webb, B. and S. (1917).
71. As for example in nursing. Abel-Smith, B., 'A History of the Nursing Profession' (London, 1960).
72. There is an important contrast here, recognised by Wilensky, between the relationship between the professions and the universities in Britain and the United States. In the United States, compared with Britain, the universities have played a much larger part, the professional associations a much less direct part, in vocational training.
73. Here again there seems to be a contrast between Britain and the United States. Millerson found that in spite of the publicity given to the Hypocratic Oath as a model, codes of ethics were both rare and relatively unimportant in British professional associations

74. Weber (1958) pp. 363–72. Rue Bucher has investigated the development of 'social movements' within a profession. 'Pathology: A Study of Social Movements Within a Profession', in 'Social Problems', vol. 10 (1962).
75. Freidson (1960).
76. Carlin, for example, in one of the studies to be discussed extensively below, found one group of lawyers who had an 'inner disposition' to ethical conduct which could not easily be explained. Carlin, J., 'Lawyers' Ethics' (New York, 1966).
77. For a similar view based on a specific case, see Ben-David, J., 'The Professional Role of the Physician in Bureaucratised Medicine', in 'Human Relations', vol. ii (1958).
78. Hall, O., 'The Informal Organisation of the Medical Profession', in 'Canadian Journal of Economics and Political Science', vol. 22 (1946); 'Stages of a Medical Career', in 'AJS', vol. 54 (1948); 'Types of Medical Careers', in 'AJS', vol. 55 (1949). See also Kessel, R. A., 'Price Discrimination in Medicine', in 'Journal of the Law and Economics', vol. 1 (1958) 20–53.
79. Lieberson's study of the distribution of medical practitioners in Chicago also showed ethnic concentration for all groups except the Anglo-Saxons who had the auxiliary status traits to fill the role of doctor for members of most races and the Jews who set about trying to acquire some such traits in the form of additional diplomas and qualifications. Lieberson, S., 'Ethnic Groups and the Practice of Medicine', in 'ASR', vol. 23 (1958).
80. Cartwright, A., 'Patients and Their Doctors: A Study of General Practice' (London, 1967).
81. Collings (1954).
82. Ibid., p. 555.
83. For example, in Britain, Taylor, S., 'Good General Practice' (London, 1954); in the United States, Peterson, O. L., Andrews, L. P., Spain, R. S., Greenberg, B. G., 'An Analytical Study of North Carolina General Practice (1953–1954)', in 'Journal of Medical Education', vol. 31 (1956).
84. Cartwright (1967).
85. This is a commonplace of most studies of the American Bar, for example, Carlin, J. E. (1966) and 'Lawyers on Their Own' (New Brunswick, 1962); Ladinsky, J., 'Careers of Lawyers, Law Practice and Legal Institutions', in 'ASR', vol. 28 (1963); O'Gorman, H. J., 'Lawyers and Matrimonial Cases' (London, 1963); Smigel, E. O., 'The Wall Street Lawyer: Professional Organisation Man' (Glencoe, Ill., 1964); Warkov, S. and Zelan, J., 'Lawyers in the Making' (Chicago, 1965); Wood, A. L. (1967) and 'Informal Relations in the Practice of Criminal Law', in 'AJS', vol. 52 (1956).
86. Ladinsky (1963).
87. Smigel (1964) and 'The Impact of Recruitment on the Organisation of the Large Law Firm', in 'ASR', vol. 25 (1960).
88. O'Gorman (1963).
89. Ibid., pp. 58–9.
90. Carlin (1962 and 1966). For a study in a different (small city) community coming to very different conclusions, see Handler, J. F., 'The Lawyer and His Community' (London, 1967).
91. Sutherland noted the importance of this culture for another 'profes-

sional' group liable to become involved in the court's activities. Sutherland, E. H., 'The Professional Thief', 2nd ed. (Chicago, 1956).

92. Blumberg, A., 'The Criminal Court: A Sociological Perspective' (Chicago, 1967); 'The Practice of Law as a Confidence Game', in Aubert, V. (ed.), 'The Sociology of Law' (Harmondsworth, 1969). See also Wood (1956 and 1967).
93. Carlin (1966) p. 66.
94. Berle, A. A., 'The Modern Legal Profession', in Honnold, J. (ed.), 'The Life of the Law' (Glencoe, Ill., 1964) p. 401.
95. Carlin (1966) p. 6.
96. For an extended discussion of the conventional position, see Merton, R. K. and Goode, W. J., 'The Client–Professional Relationship', in 'Columbia University Seminar on the Professions in Modern Society', mimeo (1962).
97. Carlin (1966).
98. Rosenthal, Dr Morris, quoted by Garceau, O., 'The Political Life of the American Medical Association' (Hamden, Connecticut, 1961) p. 172.
99. See Fichter (1961) for an analysis of the role of the unfrocked priest.
100. King has pointed out the paradox that while numerically the professions are gaining ground in modern society most are also in crisis. King, M. D., 'Science and the Professional Dilemma', in Gould, J. (ed.), 'Penguin Social Sciences Survey' (Harmondsworth, 1968).
101. In addition to the work of Huntington (1957 and 1963) see Masland, J. W. and Radway, L. I., 'Soldiers and Scholars: Military Education and National Policy' (Princeton, 1957); Abrams, P., 'The Late Profession of Arms: Ambiguous Goals and Deteriorating Means', in 'Archives Européenes de Sociologie', vol. 6 (1965).
102. Kaye (1960).
103. For a discussion of the situation in the United States, see Gustafson, J. M., 'The Clergy in the United States', in Lynn (ed.) (1963).
104. Goode (1969).
105. Parsons (1951).
106. This premium on originality is relatively unique to modern society, especially, for example, in fields like art and music. It is related to the difference between guild-type organisation and modern professional association which provides a context for individual advancement.
107. March and Simon (1958).
108. For a case in point, see Carlin (1962 and 1966).
109. It should be clear from the previous chapter that this account is an extension of the approach adopted by the Kansas researchers in their study of socialisation in Medical School. Becker et al. (1961).
110. Becker, H. S., 'The Professional Dance Musician and his Audience', in 'AJS', vol. 57 (1951–52).
111. Reisman, D., 'Toward an Anthropological Science of Law', in 'AJS', vol. 57 (1951–52).
112. Hughes (1958 and 1959).
113. Parsons (1951).
114. Ibid., especially Chapter x, and Parsons, T., 'The Professions and the Social Structure' (1954).
115. Lortie (1969).
116. Including businessmen and managers. See, for example, Nichols (1969).
117. For an example of such a controversy compare the position taken by John Whale, on the study of journalists and news in 'The Listener',

15/10/1970, with this author's subsequent reply, 'The Listener', 26/11/1970.

118. Medicine is not the least among these. See, for example, Stevens, R. (1966).

119. See Hughes, E. C., 'Dilemmas and Contradictions of Status', reprinted in Hughes (1958).

120. A reminder of this point is the media attention given to the vicar's wife who eloped with a bank clerk and made the front page of the popular British nationals on 19 Jan., 1971.

121. Goffman (1961). Mack's concept of the determinant role draws attention to similar problems in role theory. Mack, R. W., 'Occupational Determinateness: A Problem and Hypothesis in Role Theory', in 'SF', vol. 35 (1956–57); 'Occupational Ideology and the Determinant Role', in 'SF', vol. 36 (1957–58).

122. As in the studies of the Chicago school and the 'New Chicago' school. For references, see the work of Hughes, E. C. and the introduction to Nosow, S. and Form, W. H. (eds.), 'Man, Work and Society' (New York, 1962).

123. This is occupational licence in Hughes' terms. Hughes, E. C., 'The Study of Occupations', in Merton et al. (eds.), 'Sociology Today (New York, 1959).

124. As, for example, in the arguments advanced in defence of status professionalism at the end of the 19th century. See Chapter 2.

125. Whitehead (1942); Sorokin (1947).

126. For a review of some of the problems this has caused, see Birnbaum, N., 'The Sociological Study of Ideology (1940–1960)', in 'Current Sociology', vol. 9 (1960).

127. Dibble has termed this a contrast between the parochial and ecumenic concerns of an occupation. Dibble, V. K., 'Occupations and Ideologies', reprinted in Curtis, J. E. and Petras, J. W. (eds.), 'The Sociology of Knowledge' (London, 1970).

128. Kuhn, T., 'The Structure of Scientific Revolutions' (Chicago, 1962).

129. For example, Gilbert, D. L. and Levinson, D. J., 'Ideology, Personality and Institutional Policy in the Mental Hospital', in 'Journal of Abnormal and Social Psychology', vol. 53 (1956); Sharaf, M. R. and Levinson, D. J., 'Patterns of Ideology and Professional Role Identification among Psychiatric Residents', in Greenblatt, M., Levinson, D. J. and Williams, R. H. (eds.), 'The Patient and the Mental Hospital' (Glencoe, Ill., 1957); Strauss et al. (1964); Armor, D. J. and Klerman, G. L., 'Psychiatric Treatment Orientations and Professional Ideology', in 'Journal of Health and Social Behaviour', vol. 9 (1968).

130. Elliott (1971).

131. Mills, C. W., 'The Professional Ideology of Social Pathologists', in 'AJS', vol. 49 (1943). The ideology of the social worker could be said to have similar consequences. See Halmos, P., 'The Faith of the Counsellors' (London, 1965).

132. Chomsky, N., 'The New Mandarins' (Harmondsworth, 1970).

133. Halloran, J. D., Elliott, P. and Murdock, G., 'Demonstrations and Communication: A Case Study' (Harmondsworth, 1970).

134. Compare, for example, the two studies cited above which both investigate work as a 'central life interest': Orzack (1959), Dubin (1956). See also the work of Gerstl, J., 'Determinants of Occupational Community in High Status Occupations', in 'Sociological Quarterly', vol. 2 (1961);

'Leisure, Taste and Occupational Milieu', in 'Social Problems', vol. 9 (1961).

135. The Church is one of the clearest examples. Fichter (1961).
136. Morse, N. C. and Weiss, R. S., 'The Function and Meaning of Work and the Job', in 'ASR', vol. 20 (1955). See also Havighurst, R. J. and Feigenbaum, K., 'Leisure and Life Style', in 'AJS', vol. 64 (1959).
137. More recent work by Kohn and his associates on the relationship between class position and value orientation has come to similar conclusions: Kohn, M. L., 'Class and Conformity: A Study in Values' (Homewood, Ill., 1969); Kohn, M. L. and Schooler, C., 'Class Occupation and Orientation', in 'ASR', vol. 34 (1969).
138. Gerstl (1961).
139. Blauner, R., 'Alienation and Freedom' (Chicago, 1964).
140. Hickson and Thomas's (1969) attempt to derive a scored Professionalisation Scale from the formal features attributed to various professions can be seen as the apotheosis of this approach.
141. Gouldner (1971).
142. A striking example of this convergence can be found in the recent report of the Monopolies Commission on Restrictive Practices in the Professions. As noted in Chapter 1, this tackles the problem of definition by citing a list of references which replicate almost exactly those to be found at the start of any sociological work on the professions (including this one). Monopolies Commission (1970). Another example of convergence is the use made of Lewis and Maude's (1952) avowedly polemical work.
143. Most notably Greenwood, E., 'Attributes of a Profession', in 'Social Work', vol. 2 (1957).
144. Merton et al. (1957), Gee and Glaser (eds.) (1958).
145. For a useful typology of professional associations and an account of their structure, see Millerson (1964).
146. In other words, it remains to be established whether individual dynamics are so significant for those in occupations and social strata which do not themselves involve the expectation of individual advancement.
147. See pp. 108–12 above.
148. See above, p. 100.
149. See above, p. 96.
150. For the statement of the general position from which this view is taken, see Berger, P. and Luckman, T., 'The Social Construction of Reality' (London, 1967).

5   The Professions in Society

1. On the unity of other élites, see Lupton, T. and Wilson, C. S., 'The Social Background and Connections of Top Decision Makers', in 'Manchester School', 27 (1959) 30–51.
2. Jencks and Riesman's study of the changing American academic illustrates this development in one field. Jencks, C. and Riesman, D., 'The Academic Revolution' (New York, 1968).
3. See, for example, the discussion in Baran, P. A. and Sweezy, P. M., 'Monopoly Capital' (Harmondsworth, 1968).
4. A point made by Herbert Gans in relation to a specific case in 'The Levittowners' (London, 1967).

5.   See, for example, Everett Hughes' discussion of the part played by statisticians in 'Men and their Work' (Glencoe, Ill., 1958). For a personal account, see Speer, Albert, 'Inside the Third Reich' (London, 1970).

6.   A case made out in the United States by Milton Friedman and Simon Kuznets, 'Income from Independent Professional Practice' (New York, 1954). The recent activity of the National Board for Prices and Incomes and the Monopolies Commission in Britain shows that professionalism and the economic ideology of contemporary capitalism are not in complete harmony.

7.   A point noted by King, M. D., 'Science and the Professional Dilemma', in Gould, J. (ed.), 'Penguin Social Sciences Survey, 1968' (Harmondsworth, 1968).

8.   On women, see Zapoleon, M., 'Women in the Professions', in 'Journal of Social Issues', vol. 6, no. 3 (1950) 13–24.

Select Bibliography

This bibliography includes only some of the more important general discussions of professions, professionalism and professionalisation. References on more specific topics are provided as each subject is dealt with in the text.

Becker, H. S., 'Some Problems of Professionalisation', in 'Adult Education', vol. 6 (1956).
 'The Nature of a Profession', in '61st Year Book of the National Society for the Study of Education for the Professions' (Chicago, 1962).
Ben-David, J., 'Professions in the Class System of Present Day Society', in 'Current Sociology', vol. 12 (1963–64).
Caplow, T., 'The Sociology of Work' (Minneapolis, 1962).
Carr-Saunders, A. M., 'Professions : Their Organisation and Place in Society' (Oxford, 1928).
 'Metropolitan Conditions of Traditional Professional Relationships', in Fisher, R. M. (ed.), 'The Metropolis in Modern Life' (New York, 1955).
 and Wilson, P. A., 'The Professions' (London, 1933).
Durkheim, E., 'Professional Ethics and Civil Morals' (Glencoe, Ill., 1958).
 'The Division of Labour in Society' (London, 1964).
Etzioni, A. (ed.), 'The Semi-Professions and their Organisation' (New York, 1969).
Goode, W. J., 'Community within a Community : The Professions', in 'American Sociological Review', vol. 22 (1957).
Greenwood, E., 'The Attributes of a Profession', in 'Social Work', vol. 2 (1957).
Gross, E., 'Work and Society' (New York, 1958).
Hughes, E. C., 'Men and Their Work' (Glencoe, Ill., 1958).
Jackson, J. A. (ed.), 'Professions and Professionalisation' (Cambridge, 1970).

Laski, H., 'The Decline of the Professions', in 'Harpers' Monthly Magazine' (Nov., 1935) pp. 656–7.

Lewis, R. and Maude, A., 'Professional People' (London, 1952).

Lynn, K. S. (ed.), 'The Professions', in 'Daedalus' (Autumn, 1963).

Marshall, T. H., 'The Recent History of Professionalism in Relation to the Social Structure and Policy', in 'Canadian Journal of Economics and Political Science', vol. 5 (1939).

Millerson, G., 'The Qualifying Associations' (London, 1964).

Mills, C. W., 'White Collar : The American Middle Classes' (New York, 1956).

Monopolies Commission, 'A Report on . . . restrictive practices . . . in the supply of Professional Services', Cmnd. 4463 (London, 1970).

Nosow, S. and Form, W. H. (eds.), 'Man, Work and Society : A Reader in the Sociology of Occupations' (New York, 1962).

Parsons, T., 'The Professions and the Social Structure', in 'Social Forces', 17 (1939) 457–67.

  'Professions', in 'International Encyclopedia of the Social Sciences' (New York, 1968).

Prandy, K., 'Professional People : Scientists and Technologists' (London, 1965).

Rueschemeyer, D., 'Doctors and Lawyers : A Comment on the Theory of the Professions', in 'Canadian Review of Sociology and Anthropology' (1964).

Schumpeter, J. A., 'Imperialism and Social Classes' (Oxford, 1951).

Tawney, R. H., 'The Acquisitive Society' (London, 1921).

Taylor, L., 'Occupational Sociology' (London, 1969).

Vollmer, H. M. and Mills, D. L., 'Professionalisation' (Englewood Cliffs, N.J., 1966).

Webb, S. and B., 'Special Supplement on Professional Associations', in 'New Statesman', 21 April, 1917.

Wilensky, H. L., 'The Professionalisation of Everyone', in 'American Journal of Sociology', vol. 70 (1964).

Index of Subjects

174

Index of Authors

178

179